CRY OF THE SI

Tatiana Goricheva was born in the Soviet
Union in 1947. She left in 1980 and now lives
in Paris. A Russian Orthodox, she has been
involved for many years with *samizdat*
Christian literature.

CRY OF
THE SPIRIT

Christian Testimonies from
the Soviet Union
Selected from the Journal *Nadezhda*
by TATIANA GORICHEVA

English Translation by Susan Cupitt

Collins
FOUNT PAPERBACKS

First published in the United States of America in 1989
by The Crossroad Publishing Company, 370 Lexington Avenue, New York,
and this edition in Great Britain by Fount Paperbacks, London.

Original Russian edition NADEZHDA world © Possev-Verlag,
V. Goracheck KG, 1979.

German translation NADJESCHDA HEISST HOFFNUNG
by Lorenzo Amberg © Verlag Herder,
Freiburg im Breisgau, 1987.

English translation copyright © 1989
by The Crossroad Publishing Company.

Printed and bound in Great Britain
by William Collins Sons & Co. Ltd, Glasgow

CONTENTS

Preface by Tatiana Goricheva   7
The Historical Background by Lorenzo Amberg   22

1   The desolation of deserted ground   29
    A report by an anonymous Moscow writer of a visit
    to the monastery of Nil of Sorsk

2   "He who loses his life shall find it"   40
    Letters from and concerning Bishop Seraphim
    (Svedinsky) of Dmitrov

3   "You will see with the eyes of the heart"   65
    Letters from exile by an unknown priest to his
    spiritual children

4   "Become a shrine and a living icon yourself"   88
    Letters from Bishop German (Ryashentsev) to Vera
    and Natalia V.

5   "Everything lies in God's hand"   115
    Letters from Father Anatoly Shurakovski, and
    reminiscences of him

6   "Be filled through and through with eternity"   148
    Extracts from the sermons of Archimandrite Tavrion

Notes   154

PREFACE

In one of her novels Zoya Krakhmalnikova, editor of *Nadezhda*, declares that in Russia "all three temptations of the devil have been discredited, and the entire world has witnessed this edifying spectacle. There are no wonders any more, nor are stones turned into bread (indeed bread can be totally lacking), nor is there power over souls, only power over the belly. The mystical significance and consequences of this failure are now laid bare to the world, as is also the meaning of the freedom to renounce God. Know the truth and the truth will set you free, said the Lord. The first atheist state in history has shown the world that atheism is slavery."

There are several ways of refusing to accept such a state. Zoya Krakhmalnikova and her friends have rejected the path of political resistance, although she sees the political protester as "a true knight, a person of great courage, whose opposition to falsehood and violence would set him amongst the best in Russia today were he not smitten by the sickness of the times [lack of faith] which reduces his talent and chains his spirit." This is how Zoya Krakhmalnikova sees the dissident, who finds rejection easier than affirmation. Rejection merely destroys the world: what is needed today is the material to build a new one.

Zoya Krakhmalnikova herself is a builder. When she and her husband, writer Felix Svetov, accepted the

Orthodox faith, they left the secularised official culture in which they had spent all their lives. In it they had had everything: money, honour, the chance to publish, and a circle of intelligent, passionate and educated friends; in short, spiritual and material comfort. Yet Zoya Krakhmalnikova could not accept Christianity without absolute commitment. She was so filled with the light of truth which had been revealed to her that from then on she felt bound to serve it. Her poetic, philosophical and journalistic endeavours became dedicated purely to the service of God.

Literature in Russia has always played a particular role: books were a source of instruction. But in the Soviet Russia of today, where everyone learns to read and write, books have become the only source of consolation and opportunity for dialogue. Reading is an escape from the intolerable grey of existence, an escape from anxiety and from the danger of fossilisation. Zoya Krakhmalnikova has written a number of religious novels in which the spirit of Gogol and Dostoevsky is very evident. But these days the prophecies of these nineteenth-century writers have been realised in everyday life, and it is through Job's lament and the descent into hell that the ascent into heaven is achieved. In the asceticism of Soviet Russia it is easier to live on the sidelines and easier, too, to know both the devil and God.

Zoya Krakhmalnikova has become well known through *Nadezhda*. She not only collected the texts but assembled them and added comment. She copied them herself so that no one else would be exposed to the danger of imprisonment. The typed texts were put together in Moscow, then smuggled to the West, printed in Frankfurt and – again by devious illegal means – sent back in large editions to Russia. In one of her letters to the West Zoya writes about this process: "Texts and witnesses to Christ, about the life of the Church and about the reality of this life become appreciably more valuable from an apologetic viewpoint if they appear in printed form, for publication shows the reader that the text is acknowledged as having real worth by someone other than the writer. Publication is in itself of spiritual benefit. I can also tell for instance to whom I should give a printed copy of Nadezhda and who would benefit more from a typed one."

Thus Zoya Krakhmalnikova does not see herself as a political dissident, for that path did not appear to her sufficiently "transparent". This means that *Nadezhda* never contains political comment or suggestions, even in reports about present-day martyrs. The texts are "pure water", capable of quenching a reader's spiritual thirst, indeed even that of the KGB officer who conducted Zoya's last house search. As he thumbed through her papers he suddenly paused, began reading and finally said, "If only my children could read this. Why don't they have access to such literature?" Unwittingly he had been reading from a volume of Nadezhda, which was precisely what he had come to arrest her for. She had long been prepared to take up her cross, and concluded her statement before the court with the sentence, "Thanks be to God for everything". She was sent into internal exile for five years.[1]

The second millenium is drawing to a close, yet in 1988 Russia celebrated the thousandth anniversary of its baptism. End and beginning merge into each other according to the profound and paradoxical laws of eschatology. In our apocalyptic twentieth century it could be said that the frontier between heaven and earth has become blurred.

What binds them together is more readily perceptible, and their interdependence is clear. Berdyayev wrote of a new "Middle Ages". Humanism and the philosophy of the Enlightenment have long served their purpose and today the free European consciousness is no longer looking for a scapegoat. Essentially there are no classes in Europe any more: the poor are rich enough and the rich are troubled. There are no longer any criteria of race, indeed it was Cambodians who were murdered en masse in Cambodia, not Jews. And in Russia it was the Russians who killed their own kind. Who would risk openly endorsing racism today, in an age of such enlightened values? But why then the two world wars? Why then the gulags and the genocide which have never been seen in human history in such degree before? How is it that something which had previously seemed so monstrous that it was only expressible in terms of literary symbols has now become the prosaic reality of everyday life? "The eternal cold of hell" has transformed itself into the absolutely real ice wastes of the Kolyma and the Tundra in which millions of people have perished. The chant of Shadrach, Meshach and Abednego before the burning fiery furnace (Dan. 3) is now part of life, part of everyday experience in the camps, where the flames are humiliation and filthy language. Present-day martyrs are often reminded of liturgical prayers and of the words of the ascetics and the holy Church Fathers, for it is precisely in the camps that the reality of the old Christian tradition has been rediscovered. "Do you remember how we three read the Sticheron (the hymn) and the words of St Basil the Great on the Day of the Forty Martyrs? 'Winter is harsh, but paradise is sweet, the frost is agonising, but eternity is blessed" ' (Anatoly Shurakovski).

A secular humanism far removed from God can never be revived, yet man is indeed at the centre of things; as microcosm he becomes the focus of all cosmic movements and forces. Moreover he is stronger than all systems, stronger than any possible external circumstance. The camp literature makes this all so clear: throughout the writings of Solzhenitsyn, Panin or Shifrin we find descriptions of people who in seemingly hopeless circumstances have in some miraculous way been saved. Thus thanks to the miracle of prayer Dimitry Panin, author of *The Notebooks of Sologdin*, survived an illness which consumed him for forty days.

Such examples of healing and deliverance have existed since time began and in every society, but our century is applying a new set of values. What was reckoned in the nineteenth century as the experience of a few individuals (think for instance of the personal experiences of Dostoevsky's heroes) has meanwhile become the norm in Russia. Raskolnikov, the Karamazovs, Marmeladov or Prince Myshkin are not definable by social or political criteria. Their freedom is constant and unlimited: it comes from within yet also from above, from God. The horizontal tapestry of events – despite its rich meaning in Dostoevsky – is always secondary. Under the terms of the compulsory asceticism of Soviet Russia the horizontals have become verticals and the exception the rule. In fact if we compare the Soviet Union with the West we see those people in the "free" world confronted with an infinite number of possibilities. Theoretically they are all available to them, but that is precisely why they evade a decision. Overwhelmed by a vast quantity of information, they are unable to identify and choose their one and only genuine melody. The "dilemma of choice" paralyses people existentially. In the Soviet Union it is the other way round: there are no possibilities. Nearly all are blocked, forbidden even in dreams, and this is why the desire for miracles is so great. And it is precisely where a miracle is expected that it occurs. *Nadezhda* conveys this atmosphere of miracle excellently, the childish trust of the people which so fills the Russian Church. Zoya Krakhmalnikova and all of us, as neophytes of the Orthodox Church, can learn from the people of this church who are so little educated yet at heart so wise.

Today there are particular trials imposed upon the Russian Church, but this brings it strength as well as a real and total awareness of the presence of the Holy Ghost. This can be seen for instance in the numerous conversions which are now taking place and in the active existence of Russian monasticism, also in the unbroken tradition of the startsy[2] and the spiritual leadership of the father confessor. The Church is a living pulsating reality. The texts in *Nadezhda* never betray a cold or hostile attitude towards the Church.

Each of the editions of *Nadezhda* begins with sections headed "Tradition" and "Church Fathers". The remaining half of the volume is then devoted to matters concerning our own time, such as "Questions of Orthodox Priesthood", or "Individual Russian Experiences", or "Witnesses to Faith in the Twentieth Century", and to the problems of contemporary Orthodox culture. By no means is there any gulf or contradiction between these two halves. The tradition of the Church fathers is not presented as a dry compulsory prelude to each new item dealing with contemporary matters. On the contrary, these first and second halves are bound by the same spirit, the spirit of obedience and of daring. This organic link between tradition and the present is another good example of an old truth: in the Church it is not thought that progress is produced by dialectical interaction between the old and the new or between tradition and revolution. It is this dialectic which undermines the rootless tradition of Enlightenment in the West. The Church, however, sees tradition not as something to be overcome but as something which presents itself to us through continuous revelation.

Tradition and the present-day are the icons of Church experience. In the icon there is no shadow: light comes from an invisible celestial source and extends softly over the whole surface of the image. In an icon even hell is filled with light: to paint an icon there is no need for "negative" black lines and areas. So too is the life of Christ, which proceeds from strength to strength, from light to light, from abundance to abundance, and which seeks to avoid the "negation of negation", the swing between love and hate, between boredom and diversion. Only love "never faileth" (1 Cor. 13:8). It unites all affirming forces and transfigures all negative ones.

A "normal" drawing takes shape by applying dark lines to a white background, providing delineation and determination. But the painting of an icon is quite different, for it starts from the opposite principle: here a dark background lightens the image and articulates it by means of points of light. Thus the cosmos is formed from chaos and "deep calleth unto deep" (Psalm 42:8). The deep of the darkness is transformed into a sea of light. The parallel lines of tradition and present-day meet in infinity, at the point of love.

"Your monastery is Russia", Gogol once wrote to a friend. How are we to understand that? In Orthodoxy there has never been an unbridgeable gulf between monasticism (the spiritual aristocracy) and the believer: both are equally bound to avoid all spiritual compromise and each Christian must take up his cross without self-justification or self-pity and pass through the narrow gate.

"The kingdom of heaven suffereth violence, and men of violence take it by force" (Matt. 11:12). This is why great emphasis is laid on asceticism, prayer and fasting. But asceticism is not only required of monks. Prayer maintains the world, which is not only bathed in tears but also in the Logos and the uncreated light of Mount Tabor. The Church Fathers said, "Birds fly, fish swim, but man prays". The praying man, "homo orans", precedes "homo faber" or "homo sapiens".

In the history of the Church there is an obvious correlation between persecution and the strength of monastic life. In the 1930s when all monasteries were closed and most monks shot or sent to Siberia, martyrdom compensated for the lack of monks. Now that the persecution has become less horrifying the few open monasteries are regaining their intellectual force and are once again becoming the central focus of spiritual activity in Russia.

The nature of this correlation is easy to understand: each genuine monk is a martyr, a witness, dying and rising anew every day. His is a spiritual battle far more inexorable than any battle in the world outside. It not only involves testifying against the persecuters, but is also a mystical spiritual condition. "Give your blood, receive the spirit", wrote the Christians of Alexander Ogorodnikov's seminary in the samizdat journal, *The*

Community. Although they were not monks they nevertheless became witnesses to faith and prison martyrs. Even outside the prisons many Christians in the Soviet Union have to fight daily for their faith: they can be called the martyrs of life.

A Church with neither martyrs nor genuine monks is badly placed: it is condemned to death.

The maximalism of the Gospels pervades all the testimonies assembled in *Nadezhda*. It can be seen for a start in the treatment of the liturgy.

The Orthodox liturgy is the daily and hourly occurrence of salvation, a genuine dying with God and rising with him, indeed becoming God. It is a liturgy which has never been reduced to a mere "gathering of believers" where at best the Holy Scriptures are read and perhaps also other material, sometimes concerning the politics of the day.

The divine drama, with the creation of the world, the expulsion from Eden, the weeping of the Israelites beside the waters of Babylon, the presentation of Christ in the temple, the ascension into heaven, and many other events are all taken so seriously in the liturgy that it seems to the participant that these are taking place at that very moment. Thus the liturgy becomes the source of inspiration and a celebration of our whole existence. The festive theophany in words, gestures and images comes together to form a ritual which sanctifies the focal points of our lives, such as birth, death, work, eating. Even the less important moments of our lives are blessed by such solemnity. Their triviality falls away and each person becomes Adam, naming things anew.

The liturgy is the unity of the ethical with the aesthetic, a unity arising through the direct manifestation of the sacred. This is recognisable in every movement, and there is no need for a mediator to make one aware of it: "In the sacred you can glimpse an austerity, an invincibility and invulnerability, and at the same time mildness, freedom, and compassion; it is a sort of enchantment which halts all motion and a sort of attraction which is liberating."[3] And with the glimpse of the sacred there is also the music of the sacred, or better – analogous to the "momentariness" of that glimpse – the call or "cry" of the sacred. This expression is used by the Church Fathers for liturgical song, as for instance by Gregory of Sinai: "Song is an indication of the cry of the spirit from within". In the ascetic practice there are precise definitions of this, such as the way the movements of the heart become attuned to the movements of song. A just life is in itself a song.

"God commands that your life be a psalm that does not arise from earthly sounds but receives its purity and clarity of tone from the celestial heights" (Gregory of Nissa). And if the icon can justly be called a theology of colour then by analogy church song can be considered as a theology of sounds.

The whole liturgy is a glimpse and a "cry of the spirit from within". That is why time is so completely and so particularly filled in it and space is determined by personality and commitment. That is also why the liturgical experience can help us to master the present-day tendency so aptly described by Max Picard: "In this world space does not exist any more: everything is possible everywhere, people are the same everywhere, you can remain at one place yet at the same time be in flight: space is filled with the same possibilities everywhere, it has been abolished."[4] This "tourism", wanting to be everywhere yet being nowhere, is resisted by Orthodoxy through the place of worship, the place where man is no longer divided from God by empty opportunity but is warmed, received and sanctified.

That explains why the authors in *Nadezhda* never tire of praising the beauty of the house of God and its particular atmosphere, and why others who have been robbed of it are constantly mourning its loss. In Orthodoxy there has never been the strong urge for proselytisation that there is in Catholicism, probably because it prefers to keep to the concretely familiar, conveying warmth and security, rather than push out towards the strange and new or to strive for the abstraction of human love.

Today the liturgical conception of time is as badly threatened as that of space. We "never have time". We live in an age of rapid action (the Church Fathers said, "Demons are fast but not easy"), and the rate at which we live is relentlessly increasing. Paul Virilio talks of the "aestheticism of disappearance" and even founds a science of speed called "dromology".[5] Man can no longer be master of time, for this is entirely dominated by computers. He is in a state of distress, for at any moment he can become the victim of inhuman, mechanical or occult powers; he is hostage to an anonymous fortune. There is a prophecy of Ezekiel where God wishes to bring dry bones to life again (Ezek. 37:5), and the time has come when these prophecies are coming true. Our arid souls can be revitalised by means of the Church calendar, which is decked out with numerous festivals and events. Here time does not run in a homogeneous monotonous grey, where an individual is either at work or is forgetting himself in senseless enjoyment, but is represented by the uniquely constituted calendar of the saints and sacred history. And the latter is by no means at an end, but is still being written by the people of the Church.

When reading in *Nadezhda* the letters of priests in exile you are repeatedly made aware that despite difficult circumstances (to put it mildly), it is the Church feast days which determine the daily life of those in exile, enriching it and at the same time giving it firm anchorage. God's time cannot be hurried, and it triumphantly resists the hyper-time of our century.

The writers in *Nadezhda* are people of the Church and of the liturgy, encountering God's death and resurrection every day. Hence they have no fear of persecution, or of cold or hunger and imprisonment. There is no mood of complaint in their letters, nor even detailed descriptions of their sufferings. This is not merely the result of censorship (which applies to most of these letters), but also because these priests do not see themselves as "heroic", and have no wish to push themselves forward. (Is this perhaps the reason why Orthodoxy does not have "Confessions" like those of St Augustine?) Humility gives these lines their even rhythm, and they are filled with an abiding sense of peace.

When I read these accounts I often catch myself thinking that the time of the Soviets has done nothing to alter the lives of these people fighting for their faith, so accustomed are they to hunger, to waiting, and to the exercise of humility in defence of their beliefs. But the difference today is that, as already stated, they are no longer on their own: events have changed the personal individual eschatology into a general and "apocalyptic" one. As throughout the whole of *Nadezhda*, this mood of apocalyptic consciousness is peaceful and dignified. Wonder and beauty move these writers with gratitude.

Even when the priest is denied the possibility of celebrating the liturgy he still remains a liturgist, transforming the whole cosmos which is so urgently awaiting deliverance into a single church. Forest, sea, clouds – all these become the house of God. "The sea, again the sea, commanding, powerful, boundless, and majestic. I see it now as I used to see it in those days when we were all so close, in those days now gone when we shared such joy and love. Then I see it again, but differently, it does not look the same, looks dark and cold and black – but still it is the sea. I am enfolded in the protection of him who leads me on the path which is right." This was written by Anatoly Shurakovski from Solovki, which was once a well-known monastic island in the White Sea but which was later used for many decades as a penal colony. All that remains is the liturgy of nature.

A tree, a lake, or the wind are what inspire the trust of those in exile, and they bring to life the most prosaic objects with endearments. The letters of Bishop German show that his whole world is determined by emotion and pity, and his use of the diminutive adds sentiment to his description of things. He talks of a "little packet", "a tiny little bit", a "tiny egg", or "a little icon". But this does not make his writing sentimental or weak. He expresses not so much the soul as the spirit: "Our spirit must free itself from its righteousness, however pure and ideal it may seem to us, and must come to terms with God's just will. But God's will constrains our souls and is difficult to endure."

In the apocalyptic view everything is reversed. The logic

of Christian truth is constantly outraging the world. You must even free yourself from your own righteousness. Even the fact that there are fewer churches is turned to good account: you yourself are now the house of the Lord: "Now that entry to many shrines has become difficult, be this shrine and a holy icon yourself", declares Bishop German to his spiritual children.

Popular theology follows the same line, as expressed for instance in the view and convictions of pious church-going women: "Not a hair of your head will be touched unless it is God's will". Trust in the Lord, and the patience of the wise will crush the power of the Soviets, a patience without hysterical nostalgia, without Utopian projects or wild swings of opinion from "right" to "left", without haste (but also without im- mobility) and with inner vigilance. As it is said in Revelation: "Here is the patience and the faith of the saints" (Rev. 13:10).

Kierkegaard said that God is a musician who likes to hear pure sound. To discern this sound is now difficult. "Every idle word that men shall speak, they shall give account thereof in the day of judgment" (Matt. 12:36) is a warning even more valid and stringent today. Too much is said and too little done in the modern church.

The "cry of the spirit" to be heard in the *Nadezhda* accounts will please God as much as it has pleased its discriminating Russian readers. These texts are addressed to people in all sorts of very different walks of life: the "aristocracy of the spirit" (the monks), the "aristocracy of the mind" (the newly converted intellectuals), the ubiquitous old ladies, and also the Soviet bourgeoisie so keen to be in fashion.

Preface

My plea to the Western reader is: please do not read these texts without prayer. And in your prayer remember the Lord's servant Zoya Krakhmalnikova.

TATIANA GORICHEVA

THE HISTORICAL
BACKGROUND

The journal *Nadezhda* is subtitled *Christian Reading*, linking it with a monthly publication of this title which was issued by the Petersburg Religious Academy between the years 1821 and 1917. In 1978, in a totally different set of social and intellectual circumstances, Zoya Krachmalnikova revived this tradition of publishing religious texts. In the forcibly secular state of today such publication has the function of fulfilling all sorts of very different theological and religious needs. In an environment where religious material can hardly be published at all and is scarcely available such texts will be catechetic as well as a source of biblical interpretation, pastoral exhortation and, at the same time, commentary on contemporary cultural phenomena; they will also offer access to writings of the Church Fathers as well as information about modern movements in western theology. In short, they will promote a broadly-based Christian education. This is the achievement of *Nadezhda* in the last ten years. Today in the Soviet Union having a mission – and here the inner mission is meant – is to a great extent a matter of keeping memory alive and in the widest sense fighting the tendency to forget. The texts which Tatiana Goricheva has selected from the extensive material contained in the fourteen *Nadezhda* volumes are spiritual witnesses to the most recent events in the Russian Orthodox Church. From imprisonment and exile two bishops and two priests write to their communities, their spiritual children and their families.

The period when these letters were written runs from 1917 until the end of the 1930s. All religious denominations, but especially the Russian Orthodox Church, have been subject to consistent persecution since the Revolution. In 1922, after the closure of theological seminaries and academies, the government called on the Church to hand over all valuables and to give the proceeds to the starving in the Volga area. When Church leaders and believers refused to give up the church plate as well, the State answered with confiscation and show trials. In the same year the so-called "Living Church" separated from the "Patriarchate". This "left schism", led by the parish priest Alexander Vvedensky, proclaimed a new ecclesiastical administration on its own authority. Like other analogous movements it enjoyed the backing of the State which approved of any weakening of the Patriarch Church, but it had little support from the clergy and most notably the people. Benjamin, the Metropolitan of Petrograd, who had excommunicated Vvedensky, was brought before the court on trumped-up charges and was executed in 1922 along with three others accused with him. By the end of 1923 66 bishops and over 8,000 parish priests, monks and nuns had already been arrested or banished, mostly because they had remained loyal to the Patriarch Church. This persecution, as well as the death of Patriarch Tikhon, lead in 1925 to a general upsurge of piety, and even in parish churches the services followed the monastic rules.

When the successor ordained by Tikhon was arrested the administration of the Patriarch Church was taken over by Metropolitan Sergei (Stragorodsky), 1867-1944. In 1927, with the aim of saving at least the ecclesiastical structure and organisation from destruction, he wrote a declaration of loyalty to the Government. Later made Patriarch, he hoped that a conciliatory attitude would encourage concessions from the State. Although many priests and believers accepted this declaration as a necessary compromise if the Church were to survive at all, there was a second schism from the Patriarch Church. This was a number of groups forming the "right schism", who accused Metropolitan Sergei of having betrayed the Church. Amongst these was Bishop Seraphim (Svedensky) of Dmitrov, one of the authors of the letters in this volume.

Despite Sergei's declaration a new wave of Church persecution began in 1929 at the same time as the collectivisation of agriculture. A law was passed intended particularly to increase the control of the State over the Church communities and especially forbidding them any social, educational or charitable activity. The country priests, whose dire poverty had been proverbial even before the Revolution, were classified as rich farmers (Kulaks); they were robbed of their rights as citizens and, by means of oppressively high special taxes, of their means of subsistence. Hundreds indeed even thousands of churches were destroyed, icons and liturgical books were burned, and church bells melted down. After a period of relative calm in 1934 and 1935, when many bishops and priests were temporarily released, there was a further strong wave of persecution after 1936 which was maintained until 1941. All church groups were affected. The monastic communities which had numbered over a thousand before 1917 were liquidated and in the whole country only a few hundred churches were open for fifty million believers. An American church historian has concluded on the basis of cautious estimates that between the Revolution and 1941, eighty to eighty-five per cent of the clergy, that is, over fifty thousand people, had been executed or arrested.[1] As far as bishops are concerned, a list of 272 names (not including those of the left schism) of those who died in captivity has been put together in a survey published in Paris.[2] Very few of those imprisoned survived. Bishop Afanasy (Sacharov), 1887-1962, concluded at the age of 68 that, "On June 27 1954 I will have been a bishop for 33 years. During this time I served my diocese for 33 months. I was free but not exercising my duties for 33 months, I was banished for 76 months, and spent 254 months imprisoned with forced labour"[3].

The information we have about the authors and recipients of the letters in this volume is scanty. The precise reasons for their arrest and the terms of their imprisonment are also little known. This can be explained on censorship and security grounds, but it is also bound up with the personality of the writers, who always emphasise their relationship to God and to their community far more than their suffering. These letters are not to be seen as a documentary or literary treatment of Stalin's years of terror, such as is found in Solzhenitsyn's *Gulag Archipelago*, or *One Day in the Life of Ivan Denisovich*, nor do they have that distressing immediacy of a Varlam Shalamov in *Tales from Kolyma*.

These vivid testimonies lack any sense of indignation, accusation or self-justification. The writers return repeatedly to the images and religious expressions of the Slavonic Holy Scripture and the prayers of the Eastern Church, particularly the poetry of the Liturgy. Peacefulness and humility, and also regret over separation from the Church and their community, typify these letters, whose authors did not feel that they had been overtaken by any extraordinary fate but were undergoing the most common experiences of a Christian believer in an age of tyranny. Although the four witnesses to faith who speak here are people with their own fears and doubts and troubles, in the end they are able to stand up to death and destruction, isolation and imprisonment. The lives of all are regulated by the Church feast days and the liturgical calendar. Here we are concerned with witnesses to what could be called an apostolic epoch and there is much to remind us of the biblical Epistles and the documents issued by the persecuted Church Fathers. At the same time these texts remain within the spiritual tradition of Russia, with its focal points of liturgy, spiritual leadership (the startsy) and abiding prayer from the heart.[4]

That their representation of external reality is so scanty and that they are so absolutely fixed in the tradition of Church writing makes these letters more than documents of their time, which they so fully are: they are also a call for an inner spiritual acceptance of separation from the community. They are all linked by that blessing described by Dietrich Bonhoeffer in June 1944, just months before his execution in the Flossenburg concentration camp: "The answer that a righteous person gives to suffering inflicted upon him by the world is: bless it. That was God's response to the world when it nailed Christ to the cross: a blessing. God does not repay like with like and the righteous should not do so either. Do not judge, do not curse, but bless. Otherwise there is no hope for the world."

In the first of these collections of letters we see how the later bishop and witness to faith, Seraphim, gathers his strength for the period of suffering which is approaching: through the vivid description of his profession as monk we learn what it means to take leave of the world. In the letters of the unknown priest in exile we are surprised that he is so certain that the Russian Orthodox Church of this century, which has been secularised to some degree, cannot escape a tragic fate. On the other hand the letters by Bishop German to Vera and Natalia are the writing of a father to his spiritual daughters and they give us an insight into the way spiritual direction is given. Personal experience of isolation and imprisonment gives rise again and again to considerations of a general nature, particularly concerning suffering. Finally in the priest Anatoly Shurakovski's writings – he too was condemned after having been a committed opponent of the course taken by Metropolitan Sergei – we discover the physical and spiritual dangers which are encountered with forced labour, and are also given an overpowering impression of nature in the far north of Russia. In this respect these letters are the most human and most tragic of the collection.

These texts are framed by reports from Christians of our own days. The one in novel form by an anonymous Moscow writer takes us on a journey to a long de-consecrated shrine in north Russia, the Monastery of St Nil of Sorsk. The misuse of the buildings as a lunatic asylum is symbolic of the exclusion of faith from "normal" public life. The theme that Christianity has been made pathological confronts us again in the last of the texts in this volume, a sermon by the well-known starets Tavrion (1898-1978): "Our world is such that a believer is hardly accepted as normal. If he cannot be dissuaded from his faith he is put in a mental asylum."

Nadezhda was collected and assembled in the Soviet Union but these collections only appeared in the West. At present it is uncertain whether the liberalisation of intellectual life which has recently begun in the Soviet Union will extend to religious faith, and whether within the foreseeable future the publication of religious literature, in particular that which deals with Church history, will be possible. At the moment it seems justifiable to hope that people like Zoya Krachmalnikova, whose campaign against silence and our tendency to forget has contributed greatly to the present-day acceptance of the past and with this to the improved health of society, will no longer be punished as opponents of the State but will one day openly receive the thanks and the recognition they so deserve and which they already enjoy from their readers.

LORENZO AMBERG

The desolation
of deserted ground

A report by an anonymous Moscow writer
of a visit to the monastery
of Nil of Sorsk

Nil of Sorsk (Maikov), 1433–1508, was first a copyist, then a monk at the monastery of Kirillovo-Byelosersk. Despite his life of retirement he held strong opinions about important issues of his time, believing that free-thinking should be tolerated within the Church. He criticised the property-owning mentality of monasteries which at that time owned a third of public land in Russia. In his writings and talks he defended the idea of a spiritual monasticism which should take precedence over physical castigation. The Church should be poor and renounce all show, a monk should take the "divine scriptures" (the Gospels and Church Fathers) as his supreme authority. But at the same time the scriptures could be considered critically. These new ideas put Nil in sharp opposition to the monks of his time.

Officially Nil has never been canonised, but he is honoured as a saint, even in liturgical texts. The monastery he founded lies in north Russia, sixteen kilometres from Kirillov, north of the states of Vologda and Tcherepovetz.

Our journey began in Kirillov. It was the end of September and the tourists had long been gone. On the blue lake the waves were lapping restlessly, and in the whiteness above the church a lonely angel on tip-toe was blowing a trumpet. The chapel with an inscription "Souvenirs" was manned by a shivering elderly lady.

Nearby there was an ancient little bus filled with workers in sleeveless jackets who were laughing and smoking and swearing at one another. "Get in, we're just leaving", the driver answered when we asked him whether we could travel too. During the whole of the journey no one paid us any more attention.

We sat right at the back of the bus, on a worn, split red-brown seat. The men in front took no notice of us, entrenching themselves behind a wall of tobacco smoke, behind their talk which only they could understand, and behind their padded jackets. In this way we covered eight kilometres.

The land was peaceful and unexceptional, warming itself in the last rays of the year's sunshine. The weather was so warm that in the grass there were yellow heads of dandelion which had grown again, confusing autumn with spring; and in the north the grass is always green. Reddish seed heads of flax which had not been harvested were rattling almost imperceptibly in the wind. Out in the fields there were schoolchildren gathering potatoes.

The bus only went as far as Penkov, a village which extended along the shore of another lake. Melancholy spruce trees were intermingled with beeches already turning yellow which hung over the abandoned church and the nameless graves.

"The hermitage of Nil of Sorsk?", a woman repeated our question. "Ah, that must be the Institute for the Chronically Sick", she hazarded. "I worked there for nine years but then gave it up. It's frightening going there. From here it's eight kilometres away, and sometimes you meet bears. Once I came across a mother bear with her young and I thought I'd had it. That was in the spring, and since then I don't like going there on my own any more."

She showed us the direction we should take. Strange villages lay on our route as we walked. They were empty. Although there were no longer any people in them the entrances had been carefully barred with long grey poles, as is the custom in the north.

"Want to buy a house, a good one, not expensive? Only a hundred roubles", an old lady suggested unexpectedly as she approached us. "In the whole village there are only two old people left, both over eighty. All the others have moved into town, but these refuse point-blank. So I make an effort and come out to help them. If even the holiday-makers came and bought the houses it would be less miserable here."

Then we left the blue lakes, the hills, the empty villages and the gloomy spruce trees and beeches with their yellowing leaves. In front of us was a straight raised road with low unprepossessing bushes in the marshland either side. Beyond that was thick forest. A tall thin man approached us at speed. As he ran he bent down from time to time, picking things up and throwing them aside. When he came up level with us we could see how his eyes were darting to and fro. His head was shaved. He loped on without seeing us, into the empty villages.

The road seemed endless. It lay like a long grey thread in the middle of the uneventful marshland in which there was nothing at all to catch the eye. Only the sun's rays glinting on the tops of spruce trees gave us any sense of hope. It was hot and humid as we walked. The sharp smell of rosemary was almost enough to make us feel dizzy.

Then suddenly the road broke off. Unexpectedly there was a sharp bend, and the forest retreated. In front of us we could see a clearing and beyond it a small settlement. This must be the place we were looking for.

What surprised us at first was its dereliction and poverty, and also its desolate muteness. Instead of the high monastery walls and towers we had instinctively imagined we could only see low ruins, almost totally lacking in shape. No bell tower, no church towers, no sign of movement anywhere. As we came nearer we could see that there was no housing as such, merely a few desolate huts and crooked barns. From one of the huts there came the melancholy howl of an electric saw. As we approached we saw a man standing idly near a grey house which looked like the offices of a collective farm. It was as if he knew we were coming, as if he was expecting us. Behind him was a door with the sign, "Psychoneurological Home for the Disabled".

"Hello, is this the Nil of Sorsk hermitage?" – "Yes, that's right. Who are you and where do you come from?" We made out that we were city people keen on antiquities, which evidently interested the small stocky man. "Have you lived here long? Could you tell us something of the history of this place?", we asked him.

And how. Five years ago he had dismantled the old monastery mill himself, plank by plank, with his own bare hands. The mill had been there since the fifteenth century.

In his description of the monastery written 125 years ago Professor Sheviryov[1] reports: "Once the water-mill which the Saint had built on the stream had served all the monks. Now there is a barn there."

The towers in the corner of the surrounding walls, once part of the monastery, are now used as silos for cattle-feed.

"Near the cells there is a well with magnificent water which also has healing properties. This well is also the work of the Saint", reported Professor Sheviryov. "First he built the chapel and a cell, and then dug the well-shaft nearby."

"Yes, I've heard about this well", said the man, and he livened up. "An old woman told me about it once. She promised to show it to me but then she died. I've looked for it myself but can't find it."

It turned out that the man we were talking to was the senior official in residence. He had lived there about twenty years, having arrived straight after the war to look around and to earn himself a living, and he had been there ever since. He was keen to talk about the people who had taken the place of the monks, the mentally sick, and he referred to them as those "in care". And at the entrance there was merely the simple word "Hermitage" on a board.

"Come inside and see how we live. That's also bound to interest you." With the gesture of a welcoming host he indicated the porch. We had never been in a mental home before and were a little uneasy. "Holy Father Nil, pray for us."

As we went through the archway he proudly showed us some scarcely perceptible marks which hardly stood out from the dirt of the plasterwork. "Look, once there were frescoes here."

With these words in our ears we entered what had once

been the hermitage of Nil of Sorsk. Even in earlier times this monastery had been small and poor. When Professor Sheviryov had made his visit it housed twenty monks. But back in the fifteenth century St Nil of Sorsk had come here alone but for his disciple Innotenky and they had built their cells "a stone's throw" from each other, by literally throwing a stone from one cell and erecting the second where the stone had fallen. And the great starets Nil was pleased "with God's grace to have found somewhere which fulfills the following purpose: worldly folk will rarely visit here." He settled on this spot, having received instruction for some years from the startsy of Mount Athos on the shores of the Mediterranean. Later ten disciples joined him on the banks of the sluggish little river, the Sorka, which is almost as still as a marsh.

The monks led a hard life in this deserted and wild forest scrub. They fed themselves by their own work, had no belongings, and remained in their cells. Only on Saturdays and Sundays did they come together to worship in the church.

St Nil studied the Church Fathers and wrote his "Rules for the Monastic Life". In the winter the monastery was surrounded by an endless mass of impenetrable snow, and for six months of the year this settlement, the first in the Russian north, was covered by black night.

Today the number of inhabitants has reached a hundred: a hundred men suffering from chronic mental illness. In this small space we saw them moving to and fro, sitting together in groups or alone, old and young, handsome or ugly, silent or perpetually muttering. They too wanted to enjoy the last rays of the autumn sunshine.

We took the only path which led from one monastery wall to the other and which ended at an iron gate filling the opposite archway. Through the bars we could see fields, and it seemed as if in the space beyond another mysterious life began.

As soon as they noticed the strangers the men huddled together and followed behind us silently, like a flock of sheep attracted by something unusual. It was unpleasant to feel them behind us, and we were ashamed and ill at ease. Our escort paid them no attention at all.

"Papa dear, have you come to visit one of us in care?", somebody suddenly whispered hopefully alongside us. "No." No, we had not come to visit them, in fact before we arrived we had not even known they were there. Who knows if anyone in the world remembers them?

Then a cry was heard. We turned. From under the corner tower they were pulling out a scrawny close-shaved figure by his hands. He was barefoot and in his underwear with a sheet draped over his shoulder. The man was in a state of distress and crying out for some reason or other. "Doesn't matter, doesn't matter, no need to get upset, he's blind and almost dumb", our host calmed us. "They've taken him off, they have to." And to the others who were pressing close to us he yelled, "Go away, keep your distance!" And they fell apart immediately, all at once, like sheep frightened at some hazard.

We wanted to leave. Involuntarily and against all healthy human understanding we were suddenly filled with the fear that they would never let us out. We wanted to be done with it all, but needed a pretext. This arose without difficulty.

"Is there somewhere to eat in the village?" – "No, what do you want that for? You don't need that. Come, we have recently equipped the dining hall for the men in care. Come and try the food they eat." Our host invited us so pressingly that we could not refuse.

The dining hall was made out of a stone church which had been in the process of construction when the monastery was visited by Professor Sheviryov whose book we had brought with us. "In the place where they are now building the stone church there used to be the general cathedral church of the monks. Earlier everything had been made of wood, even the church with the grave of the divine Saint, but now they are using stone. Building has been in progress for several years and is not yet finished."

That was in 1847. Now it really was finished. We stepped into the large hall. Our escort left us just inside, went over to the woman in charge and whispered to her. There was nothing here to remind us of a church: smooth bare walls, modern lighting, small tables set for four, and chairs like those you could find in any building in town. Above these banalities of everyday existence there was a complete wall – probably the west wall of the original church where there had once been a painting of the Day of Judgement – with a picture painted on it: on a dense black background with clouds of thick black smoke billowing upwards there was a troika flying, with red horses, their manes spread out in the wind. Our host noticed our glances. "A painter from Tcherepovez did that. Nice, isn't it?"

At least it was symbolic. It reminded us of hell, of the stammer of the mentally sick, and of the terrible red-black clouds of smoke at Tcherepovez. It was under this painting that we ate. In local terms we were given a sumptuous meal: cabbage soup with a piece of pork, pilao, and a large cup of milk.

"This is what our patients eat, they get as much as this."

Our host was in a good mood and looked after us attentively. "It's always like this. Those in care are well looked after." He evidently thought we might be inspectors and was concerned not to drop his guard.

Somewhere, in this desolate ground now occupied by sick people, the remains of St Nil of Sorsk were still beneath the soil. "Do you know where the Saint is buried?" − "We know it's somewhere here but I can't tell you exactly. He's buried in a silver coffin." His whole life long the Saint had worn miserable garments made of so coarse a cloth that the threads pricked him like needles. His monks had neither gold nor silver, not even for worship. Poverty had been a strict principle at the monastery. Only the imagination of later generations could have invented a silver coffin for the Saint.

"Tell us, can relatives come and visit those in care? It's rather far from any public transport." − "Anyone who wants to can write to us and then we go and fetch them. A vehicle goes into town anyway to fetch the groceries." − "And can people write to the inmates?" − "Of course they can. Didn't you meet our postman on the way? He's also in care." − "How can we get back?" − "There's no car here just at present, but you can ride on the tractor. We'll take you if you like. I'll just go and fetch Kolya."

We left the monastery the way we had entered, through the archway with its dark remains of a fresco. An armed guard stepped aside to allow us to regain our freedom, and the group of sick men remained behind inside.

In the office two women were writing and rattling with their abacuses. They were embarrassed as they answered, yes, they loved this area. There was plenty of space, it was full of berries and edible mushrooms and they had vegetable gardens. "It's very quiet and deserted. Do tourists come here often?" – "Yes of course. Two years ago there was a couple of tourists here. They were professors from Moscow. They were also interested in the monastery and Nil." And they added, "These days you can live well here, there's nothing to be afraid of any more. Earlier there used to be a camp for criminals. It was difficult in those days."

Then Kolya came, the young tractor driver. We thanked our host and climbed into the trailer. The machine clattered swiftly away over the grey road, past the sunk monastery walls, the barn with the electrical saw and the boggy ditches with scrawny bushes, out onto the wide bleak road which led to the forest. The autumn day was drawing to an end.

Our journey now lies in the past. We understood that the Lord was not likely to lead us again to the derelict and forgotten land of the lost monastery of St Nil of Sorsk. It would remain there with its sad history, whereas we would continue to follow our own destinies. And yet there had been this day. It had happened, it has been written down in the book of life, our mute pilgrimage to the relics of St Nil. What good had it served? What did it bring us? What were the fruits of the expedition? What were the fruits of the whole of our lives, of our hopes, troubles, disasters and our searching, and our acts of faith and our prayers?

At the entrance to each village our driver jumped from his seat whistling cheerfully and removed the barrier by pushing the long grey pole aside. Once passed he stopped again and jumped out to replace it. "Why are the barriers here?" – "If they weren't the cattle would leave the village and get lost." – "But surely there aren't any people or cattle left in the villages any more?" Kolya did not answer that question. He drove us to Penkov as his boss had told him to do.

When finally we reached Kirillov after hitching a lift in a car it was already getting dark. The empty square was dimly lit by two or three street lights. It seemed to be filled with the voice of centuries of history which had intensified and wanted to give vent to sound. The light of a lamp reached up into the sky. In the blackness over the monastery tower the angel was still trumpeting on tip-toe.

"St Nil died on 7 May 1508, at the age of seventy-five. He had begged his brothers to throw his body to the wild animals and birds for he had sinned so much against God he was not worthy of burial. His fellow monks were unwilling to do this and are supposed to have dug a hole at the spot where he had lived and buried him without ceremony."

Twentieth-century humanity has met the humble Saint's request. God forgive us all.

2

"He who loses his life shall find it"

Letters from and concerning
Bishop Seraphim (Svedinsky) of Dmitrov

Nikolai Svedinsky was born in Petersburg in 1883,
son of John Svedinsky who was a priest in the
Church of the One Faith[1] at the Volkov Cemetery.
In 1902 Kolya (Nikolai) was so seriously ill that
his doctors gave up all hope for him, but he was
cured thanks to the intervention of the blessed
Seraphim.[2] A document written about his cure
contributed to the consecration of Seraphim in
1903. In 1908 as a pupil at the Religious Academy
of the Holy Trinity Monastery, Nikolai was
professed as a monk with the name of Seraphim.
After his time there he became a teacher at the
Bethanian Seminary for priests. In 1914 he
received the title Archimandrite and became
principal of the Tchudov monastery in the
Moscow Kremlin. For a long time he was close
friends with his predecessor Archimandrite
Arseny (Shadovsky). In 1919 he was consecrated
Bishop of Dmitrov, and the faithful in his diocese
had a particularly strong affection for him. In
1922 he was arrested and banished for two years

to the Siryansk area in Siberia. In 1925 he returned to Moscow, where he was representative of the Metropolitan Peter. In 1926 he was banished to Diveyevo by Metropolitan Sergius, in 1932 imprisoned again, and afterwards sent to Kazakhstan, first to Alma Ata, then to Guryev. In 1936 he was imprisoned for the last time, and in 1937 he was shot. All that the family was told was that he had been "condemned to ten years' imprisonment and forbidden to receive or to write letters".

Letter from Bishop Seraphim's sister Anna to her brother Michail

2 October 1908

Greetings, dear brother Misha!

We have asked Kolya to write to you and he has promised to do so. So now he has finally chosen his path in life. We were with him for two days at the Zossima monastery where he was spending the week in fasting before his profession as monk. We prayed together, wept, begged each other's forgiveness and also thought of you, dear brother, and wished you the same peace and joy which we were sharing. I have never seen Kolya so tranquil. He was composed, his face was unclouded, indeed he was radiant and beaming from ear to ear. He has genuinely found what he was searching for, what drew him so passionately. On 26 September, after the evening service, the ceremony of profession took place. We were all greatly stirred by it. Our brother Kolya is now the pious monk Seraphim! You should have seen him as the monks approached him after the ceremony and asked, "What is your name?" There was such heavenly joy on his face.

So now it is done, we have a dedicated praying monk in our brother Seraphim. Our hearts and souls are rejoicing. The next day we saw him after the liturgy with the Father Rector who had invited us all to tea. Our brother had spent the whole night in the church and had then received the Eucharist. Soon afterwards he went to the Gethsemane monastery with the starets who had officiated at the ceremony, and that is where he is now. Soon he will return to the Academy. After he had gone we sat quite a while talking to the Father Rector. He told us how he had been to see him during the night and had asked him, "Well, brother Seraphim, how are you feeling?" – "I feel, Reverend Father", he had answered, "as if the angels are singing all around me." The Rector feels that not everyone experiences this and that brother Seraphim is blessed with a special grace. Our dear brother asked me to tell you about his profession as he is unable to write letters just at the moment.

Your loving sister Nyusha

Letter to his brother

Sergiev Possad
31 October 1908

My dear brother, Christ is with us! I have just received your warmly sincere letter which moved me deeply and I now hasten to answer it. I thank you, brother dear, for your heartfelt wishes for my happiness. You ask me to tell you about the feelings which filled me before my profession and in the blessed time which followed it. With great pleasure I shall try to, but it will be difficult. How can I say what my soul experienced and what it now lives on? What words can express the feelings which fill my heart?

I am rich in the heavenly treasures which the generous Lord has granted me, so much so that I am genuinely unable to count even a half of my wealth.

I am now a monk. How strange that is, how incomprehensible and terrible! A new garment, a new name, feelings I had never experienced before, a new inner world, a new state of mind: everything, absolutely everything is new. I am new right down to the marrow of my bones. Oh what a wonderful and supernatural effect of grace! It has penetrated me through and through and transformed me. Please understand me, my dear brother, the old Nikolai – how I dislike pronouncing my old name – does not exist any more. He has been taken off somewhere and buried very deep, and not the slightest trace of him remains. Even if I try very hard to imagine myself as Nikolai I see nothing. I can stretch my imagination to its uttermost, but am unable to picture the old Nikolai. It is as if I had fallen into the deepest possible sleep and had then woken again. I look around me and try to remember what happened earlier, but find it impossible. It is as if someone had wiped my earlier existence from my mind and had replaced it with a completely new one. All that remains is the new life I had previously not known, and the far future. When a child is born it does not remember its life in the womb. It is the same with me: profession has made me a child again and I am unable to recall my worldly existence, just as if I had only now arrived in the world and not twenty-five years ago. Naturally there are fragmentary memories of the distant past; but the previous being is no longer there, the soul is different and also the self: I am no longer "Nikolai" but "Seraphim".

I would like to tell you how I gradually came to be what I am, or better, how the grace of God gradually brought me here. Recalling it will also be useful to me, for it will strengthen and encourage me, and inspire me when one day the world, as you write, impinges again upon me. I wrote telling you that my inner decision to become a monk took shape unexpectedly on 27 August, and then became fixed. On 4 September I spoke about my decision to the Reverend Father. All that remained then was to carry out this decision, to follow it resolutely through. To do this I had to offer myself for profession. At this point a cruel and bloody battle and a terrible emotional upheaval filled my soul. In the time before offering myself I was truly "groaning and trembling" (Slavonic Church version of Gen. 4:12). And there really are people who are so naive as to deny the existence of evil spirits! If they were faced with profession they would know all about them straight away! Evil fought to prevent me going ahead. God protect me – what I went through at that time!

I used to wake up suddenly at night, frightened and trembling. "What have you done?" the tempter began whispering to me. "Here's one who has got it into his head to become a monk! Stop it before it's too late!" Fear and unintelligible horror laid me in chains. After that a grumbling arose in my soul, a complete revolt, and a devilish hatred took hold of me, a loathing for the monks and monks' dress, and even for the monastery. I wanted to flee, anywhere, somewhere far, far away. This battle alternated with periods of unusual peace and blessed consolation, sent by the Lord to strengthen and uplift me in my struggle. These were the moments I described in my last letter as "unique, holy, precious, golden". I did not mention the other periods of trial and torment.

On 6 September I decided to go to the starets to ask for his blessing on my decision to become a monk. Something in me did not want me to go ahead and tried in every way to hold me back and stop me. I prayed to St Seraphim and then set out. I had bought my train ticket and was just about to get into the compartment when T.F. came out of the next carriage and directly towards me. Imagine, she had never been to the Holy Trinity Monastery before, she is not interested, and all at once there she was for the first time and precisely at that moment. I cannot describe what went on in my mind then. A whole swarm of feelings and thoughts filled my soul, I wanted to weep, and one after another tender loving pictures of family life arose vividly in my mind and at the same time dark and terrible images of a monk's loneliness, of melancholy, mourning, boredom and lack of courage. How infinitely difficult it was. And there was indeed a moment, and with pain and remorse I remember it, when I wanted to renounce my decision and approach her and talk to her. If God's strengthening mercy had not helped me I would have done so, so terrible did I feel in that moment. But no. Evil was vanquished. Seeing from that distance that T.F. was approaching and looking at me sympathetically I got quickly into my compartment and sat down so that she could not see me. Then the train left.

In the Zossima monastery the starets was surprised, and commanded me not to delay my offer. "Otherwise", he said, "the enemy will deride you even more." Thus with God's help I gained a convincing victory in an extremely difficult struggle. And now that weakening of purpose seems far away and stupid, a silly passing fancy, not important.

On 10 September I offered myself for profession and the ceremony was fixed for the 26th. The time till then raced past. It was like approaching imminent death. I took leave of all worldly things, of everybody I knew and they of me. I spent a day in Moscow and said goodbye to the nanny of my childhood and to all acquaintances. In short, I underwent the entire range of feelings which you experience when you die: unease, consternation, fear, but at the same time joy and peace. The nearer the day of profession came, and the more my heart grew numb and my soul trembled with fear, so the sense of merciful consolation grew all the stronger and more perceptible. As you well know, "The greater the suffering the nearer is the Lord".

Finally it arrived, that eternally blessed and unforgettable day. On 26 September I was in the Zossima monastery. At five o'clock I had to travel to Sergiev Possad.³ At four o'clock I left the monastery guest house with a fellow monk and went to the stalls where the horses were being harnessed. The Abbot himself, Father German, had to go to Possad and would travel with me. The horses were soon ready.

I went as far as the gate where Father German was to join me and waited there. All around the forest was asleep and absolutely still. After all the suffering and torment I had been through I felt eternal joy entering my soul and filling it with peace. I could feel that it had now relaxed and was in repose. Then the honourable Abbot appeared, white-haired, thin, calm, and praying unceasingly. We drove off and came to the station from where the train would take us to Possad. We arrived at seven o'clock. I looked around a little and then went to confession which was exceedingly thorough, covering the whole of my life from the age of six. After confession I joined in the liturgy, then went to my cell, locked myself in and went through an experience which, except in the hour of death, I shall never go through again. Slowly, majestically, serenely, the bells of the tower struck mid-day. In six or seven hours it would all be over.

If you knew how precious each minute, each second was! I strained so as not to waste a single moment. I spent the time in prayer and meditation, and in reading the Church Fathers. As far as the reading goes it was very difficult to concentrate. It is said that before your death you involuntarily remember everything that has happened to you. Thus one image after another presented itself to me: my youthful enthusiasms, my illness, our good and gentle loving father. Then this memory: the icon lamp shining peacefully, it is night . . . I am in bed . . . the pain is past and I am sitting up perplexed, looking at the icon of St Seraphim. Then on another occasion the light from the same lamp is shining on father on his death-bed. The coffin is there, around it candles, the grave, our sister, and you. All this arose in my memory. God alone knows what I felt and experienced at that time. The proud and conceited world would never understand it.

At three o'clock the Rector came, to encourage and console me. Then the students came. Some took their leave as you do of a dying person. What deep meaning lies in taking leave like this. They said goodbye to something which would never return, for it was buried for ever. At four o'clock the torment began. It is frightful to think back on it: an all-pervading melancholy came down on me like a cloud, and it was as if someone were sawing at my heart, tormenting and gnawing at it; impenetrable darkness and a hopelessness suddenly filled me, and there was no help or consolation anywhere. This is when the devil fights his last and most terrible battle. Believe me, without the help of God I would have been defeated. These are the moments of suicide. Yet at these times the Lord is always close and is observing the struggle, and as soon as he sees that exhaustion is approaching he sends his merciful assistance. With me it went so far that in the most decisive moments I felt an utter desolation, I was forlorn and totally helpless. But then I was granted strength: all at once I was standing in the midst of light, peace entered my soul, and Seraphim was looking tenderly and lovingly at me (you remember the little icon which cured me). Then a sort of electric shock went through me. Papa had come. I could not see him with my physical eyes but felt his presence within me spiritually. In a mysterious and wonderful way he touched my soul, being spirit himself. Again I heard his soft voice, intuitively. At this critical moment he spoke strongly to me, saying I would not regret the world as it held no attractions. Unusually strong emotion and blessed warmth flooded through me, and exhausted I fell to the ground before the icon and like a child began to weep sweet tears. The monastery bells struck six, lightly, majestically, imperturbably.

Until vespers there was only an hour and a half to go. I opened the Gospels quietly and joyfully and read, "Let not your heart be troubled; ye believe in God, believe also in me. In my Father's house are many mansions ... Let not your heart be troubled, neither let it be fearful ... I go away, and I come unto you ... for the prince of the world cometh: he hath nothing in me; but that the world may know that I love the Father, and as the Father gave me commandment even so I do: Arise and let us go hence." The bell of the Academy struck again. How this sound affected my heart! Then I heard a soft knocking on the cell door and opened it: a monk friend, Father Philip, had come to fetch me. "It is time, let's go", he said. We stood up, prayed, and bowed down on the floor before the icon of St Seraphim. Then we left, climbing the stairs which led to the Rector's rooms. We crossed these and came to a halt in the large room from where a door leads into the church. The room was almost dark, with merely the silent glimmer of an oil lamp. The door into the church was ajar and I could hear the singing of vespers. "O Lord my God thou art become exceeding glorious; thou art clothed with majesty and honour ... O Lord, how manifold are thy works!" I stepped into the large room and looked around. There was Father Christophorus, I bowed to him and he to me and we both broke into tears. We did not say anything to each other; there was no need for words. Then I went alone behind a screen at the side. There I found a credence table with an icon of the Saviour on it and a candle burning. I stood there in my student uniform and saw a hair shirt and stockings on a chair. Lord God, where have I landed? Who am I? Where am I? (You will remember how our father often used to say that.) I was full of terror and dread. I had to undress. I looked down at my uniform for the last time, touched it lightly, prayed, then recollected myself and began to undress until I stood there fully naked. My old self was now laid aside and the new one about to dress. Then in only the hair shirt and stockings I followed the evening service from my position behind this screen, facing the icon of the Saviour. Full of hope and faith I looked into the divine countenance and it looked back at me, gently and humbly. That helped, it brought peace and joy.

I can see myself standing there, all in white, the hair

shirt reaching to my feet, alone, humble, a nullity, undressed, barefoot. In the knowledge that I was nothing, that I was dust, I fell to the floor and covered my head with my hands. I lay like that for a time, eclipsed, insignificant and lost, and filled with the boundlessness and greatness of God. I sang with them "Glory be to God in the highest" and the Thrice-Holy, in the last repetition softly and muted as at a burial: "O Holy God, holy and mighty, holy immortal, have mercy upon us." Then the band of monks in tall hoods and long coats ceremoniously approached me with a measured and formal tread, carrying burning torches. I stepped out from behind the screen, and they led me to a raised position in front of the iconostasis where the Reverend Father Rector was standing at a lectern with the cross and the Gospel. "I will arise and go to my father", the choir sang in heavily subdued and melancholy voices. As I entered the antechapel which was lined with monks' habits I fell forward with my face on the floor, touching the ground with my forehead, arms spread out wide. Then . . . I can hardly remember what happened next: somehow everything clouded over and began to sway. I fell to the floor again. As I lay there I heard the words, "As a father loves his children, so the merciful God, acknowledging your humility and full repentance, will greet you as the lost son, you who do penance and bow down sincerely before him." The Reverend Father stepped towards me and raised me up. Then I swore the fearsome "monk's vow", publicly and in the face of God. After that I was dressed in a monk's tunic, and the black scapular with its white cross was laid over my shoulders. I heard the terrible and wonderful words, "I wear the wound of Lord Jesus Christ on my girdle." These words weighed heavily, and from time to time I experienced them as real.

The wooden pectoral cross was also laid on me as a perpetual reminder of the suffering and humiliation of our Lord Jesus Christ, the spitting, mocking and scourging that was inflicted upon him, his crucifixion and his death. Then the wide-sleeved outer robe was put on me, and a leather belt put around my body and a cloak slipped over my shoulders. After that came the cap and the sandals, and then a lighted candle and a wooden cross were placed in my hands. In this manner I relinquished the world. I died and entered another world, although it all took place on this earth.

I cannot describe how I felt in front of the image of the Saviour, in front of the iconostasis with its cross and candle. It is more than words can express.

I spent the entire night after my profession in a state of intense inspiration and indescribable delight. Something like heavenly music was playing in my soul, and it was touched by a tenderness so infinitely gentle and loving that it was allowed to fade, die away, and to sink into the embrace of the Heavenly Father. If someone had come to me at that moment and told me that I was to be executed in two hours' time I would have mounted the scaffold with total equanimity and without any apprehension, and would not have batted an eyelash at such a terrible death. Whether or not I was still in my body I am not quite sure. Only God can know.

On 27 September I received the Eucharist and was then taken by the starets to the Gethsemane monastery where I spent five days and five nights without break in the church, and was sustained every day by the offering of the Eucharist. During this time my level of awareness was at a height I shall probably never ever reach in my life again. There was everything in it, divine happiness and infernal torment, but more of the former.

I would like to describe the new life I am now leading as a monk, my dear brother, with the words of a monk and Church Father: "If laymen knew of all the delights and spiritual comfort that a monk experiences then no one would remain in the world outside, everyone would become a monk. But if they knew of the grief and the torment that must also be suffered then nobody would ever dare become one. No mortal man would ever be able to take such a step." That is the simple truth!

On 22 October I was made monk's deacon and now I celebrate the liturgy with the others every day, carrying in my unworthy hands the One who upholds all things, and participating in the bread of eternal life. Every day is a special day for me: what happiness I feel, and at the same time what a great and steadfast act of faith it is.

That, dear brother, is what I went through before and after my profession as monk. As I write these lines I am struck by the full force of this feeling: if the grace of God had not come to my aid I could not have borne it all. God be praised for all things!

Letters to his spiritual daughter Yekaterina Andurova

My dear unforgettable spiritual daughter Katyenka, my little golden dove! I thank you for your ardent letter.

Write stories. Consider this generally as a way of pitching your tent where you can, for this is necessary for survival. T. will tell you how I came to terms with living in the Siryansk area. If you are a grain of dust you do not need to fear the wind: wherever the grain is blown it will remain intact. But the massive oak-tree will fall with a crash to the ground, trembling, and "great was the fall thereof" (cf. Matt. 7:27). I am very pleased to hear you have spoken to my friend.

God protect you. I bless Shurenka[4] and pray steadfastly for her and for your Mama

14 December (OS) 1923

Peace be with you, joy and strength and light from the all-consoling Lord's Supper, you golden bee of God and novice Yekaterina, my dear Katyenka!

The Lord bless you for your good wishes for the feasts of the 16, 17, 19, 22, 24, 26 and 29 November.

That "day of terror" which you describe was only bad in dreams. Essentially it was a day of joy, God's day, as I now know. Perhaps that "day of terror" could help lighten your doubts about the saying, "He who loses his life shall find it." Try and study this saying closely sometime, and consider the passages of the Gospels where it occurs, namely Matt. 10:37-39; Mark 8:31-35; Luke 9:22-24, 14:26-34. In each case it is a question of renunciation. And it is even more so in John 12:24-5. Examples: you do not want to pray, not lose your life through lack of sleep, or exhaustion by too much standing, etc. That means look after your life, your health, your energy, and allow yourself some peace.

The Lord ordains all things, first when and secondly how he likes. Unfortunately you want to push ahead and hurry things, you are troubled and excited, and are calculating schedules. The hour will come without your asking. Take your time, do not hurry, act calmly. There is no need for deadlines. An unripe apple does not taste as nice. Also, take time over the decision to offer yourself for profession: let the idea mature. Why do you want to speed things up and push forward so? Why do you not allow yourself a little time? If something is not yet there, then wait until it comes, and enjoy what you already have. You cannot reach a conclusion about such a sacred and eternal step in merely a matter of months. Be sensible, and most especially be always humble. Only a Luther could take heaven by storm. Contemplate, and pause a little. Contemplation.

Visinga
11 September 1923

My dear clear-headed little daughter Katyenka! First of all thank you for those heavenly lines in your letter, "A powerful feeling fills my soul when I think that you are living in a room where you are succoured by the presence of the Lord's table, and that you are constantly face to face with the Saviour and in contact with the heavenly powers." My clever child, my truly clever child! What you said is absolutely right! The holy Eucharist has always incensed the enemy and spurned him into jealousy and revenge. The fallen angel will not tolerate such glorious radiance and raves, bellows and spits. And the subversive spray of this spittle does not always miss those who face the Saviour. The enemy is a trouble-maker, out to prevent us from gazing steadfastly for any length of time into the calm face of peace at its most profound. The wretch howls and spits into our mind's eye so that it cannot look upon uncreated perfection. Think of the terrible storm and the sinking boat in which the Apostle found himself with the Saviour. "But he rebuked the winds and the sea and there was a great calm." We must learn to wake him, my child, so that he quietens the storms which arise within us even when in his presence, so that no spray of the devil's storms can ever enter our eyes. Bear in mind the words of John of Kronstadt,[5] and then you will never be frightened or confused: "The deeper someone is in prayer then all the stronger and more furious are the temptations which beset him."

I congratulate you from the depths of a father's heart on your tonsure, for from the moment that you uttered the words, "Accept my vow to forsake the world", you had already taken the "inner" veil, which is more sublime than the external one. That is the stamp, but this is a document. Your document is presented, which pleases me greatly, and I congratulate you once again. The stamp will undoubtedly be added to it. But unfortunately it sometimes happens that the stamp is ready but the document is not. The stamp is then in a void, left hanging in the air. I have received the head-piece with its ribbon, have blessed it, sprinkled it with holy water and prayed over it, but would like to put it on you myself. But if you are desperately longing to wear it as an external token of your inner state of mind then I shall ask my friend M.F. to do it. I shall not write to him myself: you can show him these lines. But he will believe you without that. I am returning the earring to you, for the time for this is not yet ripe. I am also sending you water which I have blessed, and a Eucharistic loaf. I have not heard a word from Nyuta (Anna) but as you say, she is bound to write. Ah, my flowers: how the wind shifts them, dust presses on them, and the storm batters them . . .

Pass on my blessings to your calm and loving Mama. Her icon of Our Lady, "A quick answer to our prayer", consoles me. You can borrow the silent prayer of repentance from M. and copy it. It consists of laments arising from a desperate state of inner helplessness.[6] The same applies to the hymn, "To the Saviour bearing the cross and crown of thorns".

Please hand the Eucharistic loaf to our servant of God Klavdiya, as a source of consolation and to help her accept the will of God. I am praying for her dead husband. I am sending your nice herbarium and the recipes.

Please pass the attached note to A.Sh.

From now on you are no longer a grain of dust, but a drop of dew which is mounting up to Heaven.

The Lord preserve you from all temptation.

My beloved spiritual daughter in Christ, peace be with you, which you share in your heart with those nearest to you. I have sent you by post the answers to all the questions which you had jotted down in your little book. I had to tear out the pages. As regards loneliness what you say is absolutely true: it is doubled. Yet this can be borne as well. The holy sacraments crush it with the force of an iron hammer and fill the heart with the presence of God. I love your questions. It is difficult to answer them at depth in a letter.

Loneliness, my dear, only arises where the grace of dialogue is lacking. As soon as you have gained this then you forget your loneliness. But where it is lacking the soul should summon all its forces and cry, "My God, my God, why hast thou forsaken me?"

Pass on my blessing to your dear Mama. As you were celebrating my name-day I was with you in spirit and was much comforted by it. Why is Father . . . detained? I hope that does not happen to your Papa. What is wrong with Marussya's health? Is she better? I am pleased you are visiting her: you will learn a lot from it. God protect you.

You have taken upon yourself the act of faith of attending the divine liturgy daily. The liturgy is the fountain-head of daily life and the source of riches amidst the vanity of human endeavour. But do not tire yourself out. It seems to me that you are fasting immoderately. It depends upon the time at your disposal, but you can just as well attend the liturgy after you have eaten. After all, you have to travel by train to get there. My poor friend, you are tormenting your soul as Lot did. I forbid you to fast. You are already doing enough with the journeys you are undertaking and the travelling back and forth. You can maintain the rule of prayer while walking and travelling. Such tiredness, especially when the will-power is taxed as well, is an act of faith which will lead to the consoling mercy of the Holy Spirit.

Persevere. I am thinking of you and your friends. You are strong in my memory. I understand and pray for you. Do not despair.

Visinga, Siryansk
14 August (OS) 1923

Christ's peace be with you, the peace which passes all understanding, which reaches into the depths of our hearts and which is granted us by the Lord in return for our steadfast humility and humble patience. This peace be with you, my beloved daughter, fair Katyushka, you who do not belong to this world!

You intended to come and see me. I must tell you that your visit would have been a source of great comfort to me. But when I envisage the difficulties and stressfulness of the journey here I am deeply sorry for anyone who wishes to come. But it would never have occurred to me, my dear, to forbid you through T. to undertake the journey. Just where did she get that idea? All I told her was that she should make sure that anyone wishing to make the journey was absolutely aware of the difficulties it entails.

I am pleased to hear you are visiting my people. You write – how obstinate you are! – that despite what I said it is better to be an oak-tree even if it is decayed than a grain of dust which is at the mercy of the wind. But there are all sorts of grains of dust, and not all are carried off by the wind. There is also the dust of diamonds, sapphires and gold. Christ is a precious stone and as dust of this stone you are part of him. What is an oak-tree in comparison, and then only a decaying one!

I thank you and all my people in Dmitrov for telling me about the death of my sister. This information did not come as a surprise for it had already reached me through other mail. Grant your servant, Lord, eternal rest. But heavenly rest must first be earned by earthly unrest. A special quality of my sister was her faith, her love, her trembling awe before the life-administering sacrament. I never saw her receive it without tears. She used to weep with emotion. After the sacrament she was always filled with delight. She rejoiced, was unutterably happy and sang like a lark to heaven. One of her strengths was that she could be sustained by the holy sacrament in times of extreme need, and experienced the effects of communion at a very personal level. Now and again it was clear that she was so bold as to ask for the unattainable, and thanks to her vigorous faith she was always heard. In this respect she taught her brother a lot. Lord, may her soul rest in the peace she so often granted me. She should have chosen the spiritual path before her brother. Yet here too there is truth in the words, "The Lord is a jealous God" (cf. Exod. 20:5). Thank you for giving me details of her death. I also thank my dear beloved people of Dmitrov, who are so close to me in spirit. I carry them in my heart, for they are my first vineyard, the springtime of my time as bishop, my first flowers. With them I moved as if on wings and was never overcome by weariness. Out of friendship and not from a sense of duty I ask you, my joy, to arrange somehow that a cross be erected on Anna Ivanova's grave bearing the inscription which I prepared for myself during my time in Dmitrov. As my sister has died before me the inscription belongs to her:

> Now I am at rest and at ease
> For I have done with decay
> And bow down before life:
> Praise be to thee, O Lord!

Please pass on my blessing to your Mama. Her icon "A quick answer to our prayer" will never let her down. Give Shurenka my blessing and pass on to her my sympathy and my prayers. The Lord protect you all in the comfort of his all-assuaging grace.

My little daughter, my child in Christ!

You have entirely the wrong idea, you are totally mistaken, and are thereby offending the sacrament of the confession. Try some time to think about the following:

1. If someone who is severely ill and covered with open sores and scabs gives the doctor full details of the history of his illness and shows him his wounds, the doctor certainly suffers no harm and the patient should hardly be embarrassed in front of him. On the contrary, the doctor

would be grieved if his patient did not give him a full account of his condition.

2. Does the gardener complain or become angry when a favourite plant which has been tended and cherished begins to flower and to shed its rotten leaves and replace them with new ones?

Think, my this time rather less than clever child, about the great wonder and mystery of the confession which works through Christ: the more the sinner confides all defilement, meanness and impurity to his confessor the nearer he approaches the spiritual father and the more loved and trusted, the more valuable and beautiful he becomes. Remember: "and his father was moved with compassion, and ran, and fell on his neck and kissed him." (Luke 15:20). See, that is the mystery of the confession, the miracle of Christ's mercy. Christ loves the repenting sinner and he pours this love into the heart of the father confessor. To think otherwise is to misunderstand the confession. Your heaviness of spirit after confession comes 1) from a lack of understanding, and 2) from pride. To counter this read chapter fifteen of St Luke, three times very carefully, and after each reading bow down five times and say the Jesus prayer. Then it will be as if the leaden weight has been blown out of the fair head of my beloved daughter.

Your loving father

Visinga
24 October (OS) 1924
At the feast of the icon of Our Lady "The joy of all that mourn". May the joy of all that mourn gladden your heart and delight you! T., I have not enclosed any letter for you

as I have been in considerable pain. The heart failed its duty, and I felt I was suffocating. That can happen from time to time. I think I have already given you my view of sickness: through it the spirit is shaking the walls of its prison and destroying it in order to facilitate its escape. Man is a mystery, and his life is a mystery too. His entry into the world is also a mystery, as is his departure. How near we are to that world from whence pain, sorrow and sighing flee away.[7] We are ever nearer to it and it to us. Even the most modest absorption in prayer, in oneself, gives us an idea of the silence of that world, its inexpressibility and imperturbable stillness, its hidden voices and unspoken words. And surely the thousand-eyed starry heaven also gives us an indication of what lies beyond. Truly it is near, very near, shudderingly near. With Christ it is light, but without him it is terrible darkness.

I was very pleased to hear that you are reading the hymns of St Simeon and honouring the memory of their translator from the Greek, the priest-monk Panteleimon. He was a young professor at the Moscow Theological Academy and my unforgettable and beloved friend. He came across the handwritten hymns on Mount Athos. It was quite an effort for him to understand the Greek manuscripts. His asceticism sapped his strength, and he burned down like a candle before the Lord. I loved him, that strict monk. I was involved in his becoming a priest. He was called "Mily – my dear" in imitation of his Ukrainian accent. He died the death of a saint on Mount Athos, where he had gone for his health. When he was working on the hymns in the Academy he would often invite me to listen to one or other remarkable passage, saying "My dear friend, just listen to this . . .", and he would read a section to me, with great humility and an angelic expression on his face, meditating on it and discussing it with me, and in doing so he forgot all earthly things.

The Lord sustain you in the feelings and thoughts contained in the blessed hymns of St Simeon. You will receive answers via T. by the next post to the questions you sent. Pass on my blessing to your Mama. Protect her in every way you can. I also send my blessings to all my loyal friends. I am now in good health. Two of our people, Snamensky and Poykov, have obtained a conditional release.

Stay strong, pray often to Our Lady in all her purity. For how can we be fearful with such firm support and such protection? Ask her for purity. Only she can give it to you. Without her you will receive nothing.

For your name day I wish you peace, joy, repose, comfort, and the light of the Lord's Supper.

The wisdom of your saints fill you with understanding, for it is written: "The beginning of wisdom is fear of the Lord." It can make you quite rigid, this fear, and so chain all your limbs and paralyse you so that you can no longer move. The Lord is near, and sees right through you. "Walk before men and be thou perfect," (Gen. 17:1) he says, seeing all.

The beauty of Yekaterina[8] fill your heart, for it is written: "Blessed are the pure in heart, for they shall see God". Let the richness of your saints enrich your will with all kinds of good acts in Christ's name. Bless your Mama and Marussya for me. How is Shura? When the land is very marshy you must put your best foot forward and walk resolutely on. Otherwise you will become stuck fast. The Lord is with you.

"He who loses his life shall find it"

Letter from exile to his spiritual children

To all my beloved children in Lord Jesus Christ and whose names I carry in my heart, I send grace and the Lord's blessing. I am in the midst of a long and arduous journey involving many stages and with exhausting periods of delay. Yet the whole of this way, from Melenki to Moscow, from Moscow to Alma Ata, from Alma Ata to Uralsk and now the stretch still to be covered from Uralsk to Guryev on the Caspian Sea, is wonderful and un-forgettable. In short, it is the way of wonders, vouchsafed in response to one hundred and fifty Hail Marys. From time to time it seems as if the Lord has sent me on this journey expressly to show me what prayer to the purest of all mothers can achieve, and to show me the effect of the greeting which the Archangel offered her in faith. I believe and acknowledge that this journey has revealed to me the complete sense of security and full protection that this wonderful salutation can give. I had never experienced it to such degree before. Hail Mary! It has smoothed my path and that of my trusty fellow travellers in some of the roughest situations. It has often moved wicked hearts, and has unsettled and embarrassed those who would not be moved. These will drift away like smoke.[9] The Arch-angel's greeting has always given me sudden and un-expected help in times of the most profound helplessness, and indeed from directions where I had least expected it. As for that inner peace which is sustained in times of storm, and the inner harmony when all outside is chaos, these I will do no more than mention, for these too came to me through the Hail Mary, which deflects God's just anger from our heads and even negates the verdict of the judge and of God himself who knows our hearts. Oh what daring! What mighty support we have! He snatches us out of the fire of passion and lifts us from the depths to which man has fallen and takes us up to Heaven.

So, my dear children, whenever possible build up this firm defence around you, this indestructible wall: Hail Mary, full of grace! With this prayer we shall not fail, we shall not be burned by fire nor drowned in the sea. And when Satan, who hates us, bars our way and brings us down, then we send this angelic salutation up to heaven and pick ourselves up again. Blackened by sin, we shall become as pure and as white as snow, and our purity will be "higher than heaven and brighter than the clarity of the sun". Dead, defeated by passion, we will rise up, will live again, and will cry out in rapture, "Christ has risen! He has truly risen!"

3

"You will see with the eyes of the heart"

Letters from exile by an unknown priest
to his spiritual children

It has proved impossible to trace the name of the
author of these letters. The church where he was
active is also unknown. It is probable that he
perished in the twenties or thirties, like so many
of the priests who were arrested or banished. His
tremendous religious gifts, evident in these remarkable letters which he sent to his parish, give
grounds for hope that the Lord will be merciful
to his servant Sergius and will make a place for
his soul in the kingdom of the just.

God be praised in all things. It was on the day of the icon
of Our Lady of Kazan, at the end of the morning liturgy,
that our first "check-up" in hospital began. And it was on
the day of St Theodore the Studite that we were sent to
the "health resort". I see all this as a powerful sign from
God to us all: Our Lady has blessed the start of this affair
and the Saint has confirmed the rightness of our way. Do
not be upset, but be pleased that in times of trial we are
not without the help of heaven. Even less should you be

concerned on my account: the Lord is calling upon me to provide "the service of a man to the one God". Nothing can change this, either for me or for you, for my whole life is in you and has no meaning without you. Neither should you be distressed on your own account, for you still have the best thing of all, which many, myself included, have been deprived of: divine service in church. As my children and friends, this is my legacy to you: cherish the divine service, cherish your priests who are your kin in spirit and who are linked by the close ties of succession to our dear departed Father, priest at our church before me. Do not look for normal spiritual leadership, for the times will not allow it. Nor will you find it, or if you do so it will be merely for a moment. Look to each other, learn from each other, strengthen and console each other. "Bear ye one another's burdens and so fulfil the law of Christ". Consider that you might always be without a priest. The exceptional situation (which requires you to avoid exposing priests to danger and to be prepared for yet further trials) obliges me, your father, to order you for the moment to go less often to Confession and Holy Communion. There is no other way: accept it as the will of God. Normally you receive the Sacrament twice a month and on feast-days, but now it must be just once a month and only on major feast-days. Prepare yourselves carefully for the days when you take Holy Communion. This will bestow upon you a sense of joy you have never felt before . . . Trust me, make use of any priest who will hear your Confession. Bear the times in mind. Pray for me. However joyfully I accept my banishment I am only human, and am unable to live through feast days and particularly Friday evenings and Sundays without distress and tears. Pray for me on each of "my days", just as you have done till now. I can sense your prayers. Pray to the Lord for me that he will give me strength to present myself anew for his service, on your behalf and on your authority. You are all in my heart, you have become nearer and dearer to me. Forgive all wickedness I may have committed during the decade we shared together. I place you all in the hands of Our Lady, our Saints, and each other. From the depths of my heart I wish you happiness for the approaching celebration of Christ's birth.

The Lord be with you through the prayers of his most pure Mother, through the intercession of the holy angels, of our holy father Nicholas, Archbishop of Myra, who works miracles, of the Moscow bishops Peter, Alexis, Jonas, Philip and Hermogenes, of St. Sergius of Radonezh, Theodosius of Totyma, Theodore the Studite, and the Man of God Alexis. The Lord bless you and have mercy upon you, for he loveth mankind, both now and forever and world without end, Amen.

No longer I, your father, but other priests are now accompanying you through the sacred great fasts. "I know, O Lord, that the way of man is not determined by his own will and that it is not within the power of the traveller to lay down the direction of his steps." Yet as a man this is just what I have been yearning for, to spend these fasts, the fasts of my renewed priesthood, when the Menaion combines with the Triodion,[1] with you, my family of penitents, just as I did in the year of my ordination. Do you feel, my beloved ones, how my spirit reaches out for our place of worship, that every evening, every morning, every middle of the day, my soul is drawn to each one of you? The Lord has united me with you. I am as unworthy and more sinful than anyone, but I am your pastor and am consumed with grief at this separation from you. You are my breath, my life, my joy. You do not conceal the Lord from me but reveal him; you do not remove him from me but bring him closer. Through you I have acknowledged the Lord, in you he has revealed himself to me. With you and your authority I sent up my prayers to him. In serving you I was serving him, I saw your beauty fashioned in his likeness, and raised myself to his inexpressible goodness. I knew your sins and wept over my weaknesses, I saw how you reformed yourselves, and was ashamed, and begged him to help me reform my own sinful existence. In short, for many years it was through you that I approached him, and it was with your aid. You are my way to Christ. How can I continue on this road? With tears in my eyes I pray: "Thy will be done, O Lord, even with me a sinner". Do not forget me. Remember what I taught you, however unworthy I am. More than anything preserve the unity of the spirit and the bond of peace. Remember that for you, too, who for the present are still allowed to enter church, the hymns of the Exodus are still before you. Each one of you should return to his duty and forget what divides you: you must unite together in the Exodus! A lot can happen to you: it is the end which crowns the work. Wash and purify yourselves, and set out with one accord. My cross is lighter through the joy I feel in your repentance. I taught you as well as I was able, however unworthily that was, and the most joyful day for me was always the start of the great fast, the day of Adam's fall. Pray for me on this most important day, and also beg our dear departed Father's forgiveness on my behalf. I believe that on earth there is no separation in space. Christ has the power to bring together the things which are separated. On that day we shall all be together in spirit, and as you leave the church you will all fall down before my saints, before my angel and his assistants, and before my patron saint, and you will ask them to accept your repentance. And the Lord will renew you in my memory, and from my place here I bless you every one. And you will then pardon the sins of your sinful and unworthy priest Sergius, your father, who falls at your feet and begs your forgiveness.

With the whole of creation I rejoice and am glad in this night of deliverance: Christ has risen, and has vanquished hell! Filled with the gladness of Easter I now turn towards our church so full of light and decked with flowers and resounding with your hymns of joy, and I bless you with the Holy Cross, my beloved children and orphans, as I always used to, and I cry out with all my soul, "Christos voskresse – Christ has risen!"

Now I am celebrating Easter another way, on my own like a great sinner. This way I experience the resurrection all the more deeply, but I sadly miss that office of pastor which I had the privilege of performing on this day. My heart aches, therefore, and my eyes are filled with tears. Easter has come, but you, my children, are not with me. Not everyone would understand my feelings, but I know you can. I can sense how tears are welling in the eyes of many of you. Indeed, how can we not weep over each other on this day? We form a family not only in repentance but also in the divine service. I am not only your spiritual father but also the leader of your church, and you are not only my children but you also serve with me. Our fullness of being is that of a repenting family celebrating the divine service. Neither in myself nor in the divine service can I separate what is mine from what is yours: it has combined to form a new organism which together performs the duty of a spiritual family. I have lived through you and you through me, and all of us – through Our Lady, our saints and through the blessed remembrance of our dear departed Father – through Christ. How can we then be separated? Tell me, where is my mouth and where is yours, where is my heart and where is yours, what did I set going in our church and what did you? What I was for you is something you will all have in your hearts, but of you I say: you are my mouth, in the liturgy it was through you that I sent up my sinful prayers to heaven. You are my heart, year after year you confided your secrets to me which are now stored in my unworthy heart, so that it has been extended by your hearts and it is impossible to distinguish between yours and mine. You are my soul: for a long time I have lived through your joy and sorrow, and in my most intense moments I feel that I have no other life. My heart has been taken from me and my soul robbed. How can I then not recognise that it is the result of our sins and chiefly mine that we are deprived of our proximity to one another, and our most natural bond has been torn apart at God's behest?

As I mourn for you I weep over my sins on this great day, and in this fashion I rediscover the Easter service. Till now it was the divine service of paradise, but in it I now see the possibility of repentance and remorse. My childhood and youth and also the first years of my priesthood were spent with our dear departed Father, and it was through him that I first learned to understand Easter. His services were unusual in every way, breaking the bounds of the normal framework of hymns and readings, and at Easter it was always a very special experience. Through its sheer simplicity the service attained such depth and power of expression that it fired and shook us all, moving us immensely. Today our manner of celebration is a pale reflection of our dear Father's flaming soul. Do you remember how he used to give you the Easter kiss of peace, and how he read the Gospel and delivered the Easter homily of St John Chrysostom? Even as a child I was impressed by the way he sang the Easter Oikos. Without knowing why I awaited the Oikos with the same spiritual intensity as I did the first "Christos voskresse", and the homily and the Gospel. He sang this Oikos in such a way that its meaning was revealed, and the sense of one or other of the expressions underlined. Then amidst the delight and rejoicing of this night he would suddenly retreat into himself, so to speak, and as he came to the words, "O Master, arise, that those who have fallen may rise again", I could sense that he was inwardly weeping and sobbing. Who was he grieving for? For our Saviour? No, now I know, it was for himself, the fallen.

The Oikos is a special hymn of penitence in the midst of the jubilation of the Easter service. The most important part of the canon, the Contaction, provides the central meaning of the ceremony, and the Oikos complements and consolidates it. Then suddenly it proves to be as follows: the Contaction is confirming Christ's resurrection as victory over death. "O Immortal One, you descended into the grave, you overthrew the power of Hades: you rose victorious from the dead: Christ O Lord! You greeted the women bearing myrrh, gave peace to your disciples and resurrection to those who had fallen." But the Oikos, on the other hand, instead of reinforcing the joy of resurrection, leads us back to mourn the dead Christ: "Come, friends, let us anoint with spices the body which is a source of life but is now buried, the body which raised the fallen Adam but is now lying in the grave. Let us hasten to adore him as did the wise men, and offer him our gifts of spices. He is now wrapped in a shroud and not in swaddling clothes. Let us cry out and say: Arise, O Master, and give resurrection to the fallen ones." This hymn belongs to the central part of the Easter morning office, and it lies beyond the usual scope of the divine service. For how can we weep when the angel has already said, "Cease your weeping"? How can we beg him to arise when he has already risen? Only the soul of the truly penitent can comprehend this remarkable and magnificent hymn. Zion is now rejoicing and is glad, and we all enter it clad in wedding garments, so that with St John of Damascus and other saints we shall meet the bridegroom, the risen Christ.

Within me too I feel joy rising, and it radiates light, even though my clothing is dark and torn. Lord, I am not yet bound or cast out by the angels: I am still with them in paradise. Yet it is clear to me that this garment of flesh is in shreds. Here I can still do penance, I see the blessedness of the just and observe that Christ has risen for them. So then I weep and cry out with the women bearing myrrh, "Master, arise for me also, and let me the fallen arise."

The triumphal climax of the yearly calendar, the Easter Contaction, merges into the climax of repentance, the Easter Oikos. This is a focal point, bringing together the full repentance of the time of fasting in the midst of the jubilation of the heavenly Jerusalem, so that the light of repentance pours down from Zion over the whole of the remainder of the Church calendar. A cry of repentance breaks into the Easter hymns, a cry which penetrates into the depths of the penitent heart so that paradise is revealed. As I sit here now I am aware of the words of the Litany of Supplication as if hearing them for the very first time. "The pardon and remission of all our sins and weaknesses ... that we may spend the rest of our days in peace and repentance ... a good answer before the dreadful judgement seat of Christ, we beseech thee, O Lord." Tears, tears of repentance overwhelm me, but in my soul I can feel that joy is growing, joy that he has risen, and not only he but I also, I the fallen.

"My fathers! For the Lord's sake do not leave one another, for in these days so burdened with disaster few folk are to be found with whom one can exchange an honest word." (Theodore of Svir)

To my children, those who are still together and those now scattered, I send God's blessing on this day of St Sergius, the feast-day of our family. I will never forget the days we spent together in commemoration of my patron saint. They will remain forever in my memory as days of the greatest pastoral joy, and at the same time of a sadness which is just as deep. In the course of a year the thin rivulet of my existence has hardly reached you, but in those days you, my beloved ones, filled me with a powerful stream of loving kindness. I preserve it carefully, and it still warms my heart which is now becoming chilled with loneliness. How I now thank the Lord that my path crossed yours. I can remember seeing you as you all came flocking in: so many of you possess the gift of faith, and are continuing steadfastly in your efforts.

"See, there is so much that is good and lovely, but to a community which lives in harmony God promises eternal life." These words of the gradual hymn of St Theodore the Studite take on a particular meaning in my mind. The hours which we normally used to spend together are now approaching. Yet my family is now orphaned, and their father alone. Today you will not be coming, I will not see you, and I will be unable to give you my fatherly blessing. I bow down to the ground before you, thankful for the richness of my time as pastor which you brought me through your love. You did God's bidding and disregarded my puny spirituality, and patiently you concealed my weaknesses. For you what is promised in God's commandment will be fulfilled: "May it go well with you, and long may you live upon earth!" In the days of anxiety about our church and about my children who were celebrating the divine service with me, I happened to read the words of the starets Amvrosy[2] about the Cross in the life of man. They gave my sorrowing heart tremendous consolation, and I would like to pass them on to you, my beloved ones: "It is not God that lays a cross upon us, that is, the cross of purifying spiritual and physical suffering. However heavy the cross might be for one or other of us, the tree from which it is made is always rooted in our own hearts." Referring to his own heart the starets added, "The tree stands at the spring from which water (the passions) wells." "If a man takes the straight path", he also says, "then there is no cross for him to bear; but if he leaves it and begins to cast about on one side or another, then circumstances will arise which will persuade him back on the straight path. And it is these circumstances which form our cross. Naturally there are many different kinds of cross, and each man has the kind he needs." I would like to engrave these golden words in the hearts of all of you, my loved ones. Carry them within you, fence your spirit about with them, and they will become part of your conscience. In the place where our family sits in judgement you will be able to discover why your cross has rooted in your hearts, and why there is now suffering in our family of penitents. It is now almost a year since I your father celebrated the divine liturgy with you and have been separated from you.

Our Lord Jesus Christ who came down to earth to save us had his own worshipping family of penitents. He prayed with them, he taught them, and with them he went up to Jerusalem to meet his Passion, and finally it was with them that he celebrated the greatest sacrament of the new fellowship, the Lord's Supper. The apostles called by the Lord were bound to his person, but in being so were soon related to one another. What instructions did he give them to follow? That they should regard their "family" as divine and sent from God. "I pray not for the whole world, but for those which you have given me, for they are yours." They should be at one with each other: "Holy Father, keep them in thy name which thou hast given me, that they may be one even as we are" (John 17:11).

In love: "A new commandment I give unto you, that ye love one another; even as I loved you, that ye also love one another. By this shall all men know that ye are my disciples, if ye have love one to another" (John 13:34-45).

In serving each other: "Ye call me Master, and Lord: and ye say well, for so I am. If I then, the Lord and Master, have washed your feet, ye also ought to wash one another's feet. For I have given you an example, that ye also should do as I have done to you" (John 13:13-15). "He that is the greater among you, let him become as the younger; and he that is chief, as he that doth serve" (Luke 22:26).

In the requirement that all should live within the community, now and forever: "Father, that which thou hast given me, I will that, where I am, they also may be with me" (John 17:24).

Thus receiving the spiritual family from God's hand, being at one with it, dwelling in it in love and humility, and above all, always living within it, these are the foundations of the way laid down for us by Christ. This was also the way of our great forefathers. Moses received his "family", the people of Israel, from the hand of God. And he did not leave it even when God imposed his avenging justice by destroying Israel after the offering of the Golden Calf. He served his people to the end, for he felt that without him they could not be reconciled with God. "Yet now, if thou wilt forgive their sin; and if not, blot me, I pray thee, out of thy book which thou hast written" (Exod. 32:32).

When Paul created the new family of the "Gentile nations" in the Lord he also had in mind the first family God had given him, Israel. He endured a lot for it, and in serving it he reached the point where to save it he was even prepared to be separated from Christ: "I say the truth in Christ, I lie not, my conscience bearing witness with me in the Holy Ghost, that I have great sorrow and unceasing pain in my heart. For I could wish that I myself were anathema from Christ for my brethren's sake, my kinsmen according to the flesh: who are Israelites" (Rom. 9:1-4).

With the Lord there will be no more separate existence, all who have served him at some time or place on earth will be gathered together in his community. But how to live there in harmony must first be learned beforehand here. Being united with the spiritual family, loving it, serving it and being required always to live within it are the subjects of a Troparion which St Theophanes dedicated to the martyr Theophanes the Branded: "In offering a song up to the Lord, O Father, I pray unceasingly for my weakness, for those living with me in the community, for my brothers, so that after our lives together we may also reach God together."

My children, our family also comes from God. Do we accept it from the hands of the Almighty? Are we united in love of it? Are we also serving it? Pray to God, beg him that he might free you from your lack of cordiality so that your hearts can reach out again to each other. He will then release you from these restricting bonds and lead you out into the open. Then it will not be with the eyes of the body but with the eyes of the heart that you will see the children gathered by the Lord around you, which is your family, and in it those nearest to you. And in your hearts a song will rise as previously it did in mine at the feast of St Sergius: "See, there is so much that is good and lovely, but to a community that lives in harmony God promises eternal life." Love the family, and serve it, as our dear departed Father also taught us.

Blessed Father Theodosius, blessed Father Pimen, blessed Father Theodore, blessed Father Sergius, blessed Alexis, the Man of God: you who offer the Lord your songs of praise, pray for my weakness, for those living in community with me, for my brothers, so that after our lives together we may also reach God together. God's blessing be upon you all.

On the closing of the church

To my suffering homeless family I send my blessing as you enter the great time of fasting.

I can sense that you have been waiting some time for a

word of consolation from me, but my mouth has been closed, my spirit in despair, and my heart confused. Our heaven on earth is barred from us. Why should we not weep, lament and grieve?

"Gird yourselves with sackcloth, and lament, ye priests; howl, ye ministers of the altar; come, lie all night in sackcloth, ye ministers of my God: for the meal offering and drink offering is withholden from the house of your God" (Joel 1:13).

In moments of joy and particularly of sorrow it happens that our nature, fashioned in God's likeness, is drawn to our own kind. "It is not good that man should be alone; I will make him an help meet for him" (Gen. 2:18), said the Creator at the start of the history of mankind. Also our Lord Jesus Christ, mourning over his approaching death as he prayed in terrible extremity in the garden of Gethsemane, and strengthened by an angel, he too, in the manner that people do, sought support from those around him, from those he loved and with whom he had trodden the path of his earthly existence. "My soul is exceeding sorrowful, even unto death; abide ye here, and watch with me."

As for me, I am sinful and fainthearted, but strengthened by your prayers and by your passionate service with me in the house of the Lord. Lonely and isolated, I am all the more aware of the triviality of my existence and the limitations of my mind. To my anxiety about the church is now added anxiety for you and the consciousness of my great guilt before each of you. I find no consolation in anything, like Hezekiah: "Like a swallow or a crane so did I chatter; I did mourn as a dove; mine eyes fail looking upwards. O Lord, I am oppressed, be thou my surety" (Isaiah 38:14).

I know that you are praying for me, that as you grieve your prayers have reached the Lord, and he has shown mercy on me a sinner. The songs of repentance have also touched my despairing heart, and the words of the great Ascetic help to channel my grief in the right direction: "He who hopes to triumph over temptation without prayer or patience will not escape it but become entangled all the more" (The Ascetic Mark, fifth century Egyptian desert saint).

All that is within me is turned towards the Lord. Only he can help me, "for he maketh sore and bindeth up, he woundeth and his hands make whole" (Job 5:18).

"I am yours, save me." "Heal my soul for I have sinned against thee." And in answer the words of the ancient sage are revealed to me: "Give not over thy soul to sorrow; and afflict not thyself in thine own counsel. Gladness of heart is the life of man; and the joyfulness of a man is length of days" (Ecclesiasticus 30:21-23).

"Set thy heart aright, and constantly endure . . . Accept whatsoever is brought upon thee, and be longsuffering when thou passest into humiliation" (Ecclesiasticus 2:2,4)

Through your prayers the words of the psalmist have been fulfilled: "In the multitude of my thoughts within me, thy comforts delight my soul" (Ps. 94:19). And now with his support I shall try to write you some words of consolation and in this way help to alleviate your pain.

The judgement of God is being executed on the Church of Russia. It is not mere chance which has deprived us of the visible side of Christianity. The Lord is punishing us for our sins and is calling upon us to purify ourselves. For those who live in the world, what is happening at present is surprising and unintelligible. They still like to trace it back to causes outside the Church. But to those who live in accordance with God's ways it has all long been clear. Many controversial religious figures in Russia have not only forecast this terrible time but have also borne witness to it.

They did not see the danger for the Church as external. They could see that true piety was abandoning even the monasteries, that the spirit of Christianity was imperceptibly in decline, and that the worst hunger had already started, hunger for the word of God. To them it was clear that those who possessed the key to understanding were not using it themselves and were barring the way for others, so that despite its apparent prosperity monasticism, and then also Christianity, was drawing its final breath. The path of true piety laid down and described by the fathers of antiquity had been and still is forgotten. Also gone was the secret of the inner life and the possibility of attaining it, for "the Saint has abandoned us, and truth has been withdrawn from the sons of men." Then from outside the Church the persecution began, making our time reminiscent of the first centuries of Christianity. The Moscow Metropolitan Philaret (1783-1867) often indicated in conversations with those nearest to him that in Russia a period had begun which was similar to the first centuries of Christian persecution, and he wept for the children who he felt would have to face the coming troubles. Premonitions about our epoch were particularly strongly expressed by two bishops committed to the interpretation of God's word, Tikhon of Zadonsk (1724-1783), and Ignatius Bryanchaninov (1807-1867), "Today there is very little genuine piety, only hypocrisy," declares Bishop Tikhon, referring to the Church of his time. He forecast the gradual retreat of the Church from people indifferent to her, so that Christianity as the sacraments

and the life of the spirit would become lost to those capable
of preserving this priceless gift. A century later Bishop
Bryanchaninov speaks of the state of monasticism and the
Church as follows: "The external form of Christian piety
is preserved after a hypocritical fashion. Mankind has
renounced the power of piety and rejected it. One can only
weep in silence."

He sees monasticism as the barometer of the spiritual
life of the Church as a whole, and his opinion of its
condition is as follows: "One can say that the matter of
Orthodox belief is being conclusively resolved. The decay
of monasticism is considerable and what has happened
cannot be undone. Only the special mercy of God can halt
the spread of this devastating moral epidemic, but it would
only be for a while, for what has been prophesied in the
scriptures must be fulfilled."

"My heart is consumed with remorse as I follow the
inexorable decay of monasticism, pointing as it does to
the decay of Christianity itself."

"The longer the time the more difficult it becomes: for
to the scurrying throng who serve the world the retreat of
the Christian spirit is imperceptible, yet to those who are
attuned to it it is easily detectable. Christianity is abandoning humanity and leaving it to its downfall. Whoever is
then in Judea, let him flee into the mountains."

Many controversial religious thinkers of the eighteenth
and nineteenth centuries recognised in their own times the
signs of approaching disaster for the Church of Christ.
One must remember that this was in a period of apparent
prosperity: the monasteries did not merely exist, but were
in excellent order and a good state of health, indeed new
ones were being founded, churches built, and holy relics
made accessible. The Russian people became known as the

preservers of the pure faith and genuine piety, and it was by no means generally thought that the Church was in trouble and the end approaching. But for those who had acknowledged the kingdom of God it was different. Filled with sadness they looked around, and seeing about them no life in Christ they prophesied the catastrophe. "Only the special mercy of God can postpone it for a while."

And so it then happened. Just as a lamp flickers brightly before going out, so the Russian Church flourished briefly once again. In some monasteries in the last century the true light of Christian life was revived and extended from there to the outside world, such as in the time of the Kiev monks Antony and Theodosius and St Sergius of Radonezh. They rediscovered the long-forgotten path of the practical way to God, the path once trodden by the leading figures of the past.

In some monasteries, the most important being Optina Pustin, the ascetic works of the Church Fathers were translated, studied, and published, and on the basis of a patristic experience of God monastic practice was totally renewed. Bishops such as Ignatius Bryanchaninov and Theophanus the Hermit not only read the Church Fathers but through their personal experiences provided touching interpretations of them, thus making a powerful contribution to religious patristic literature. The monks were not understood, were derided, and accused of alleged reforms as they defended the patristic way of life against worldly Christendom. But monasticism regained its spirit, and fire was also rekindled in places where before only embers had smouldered. The previously neglected works of the Church Fathers became handbooks, and the monks of the ancient hermitages in Egypt, Thebes, Palestine and Syria were seen as providing useful instruction in life.

Finally the flames of committed Christianity spread from the monasteries into the world outside. It drew many people to the revitalised monasteries, to the startsy who were then introduced and who thereby actively participated in the ascetic tradition. Parish priests also visited the monks and were kindled by the spark of the Church Fathers which they in turn transported back to their churches. In this manner the sermon gained new life: the works of the Church Fathers were no longer seen as edifying documents of a past age but of life as such. The world drew nearer to the monastery, and the dividing wall between the two collapsed. The monastic order became the foundation of the divine service in the parish church and the faithful participated actively in it. Confession became the mainstay of existence: families of penitents arose, which were continually reconsecrated by the Sacrament. With frequent church-going and daily Communion the previous pattern of everyday Christianity was fundamentally changed.

Since the time of St Sergius the Church had not experienced such a vital new upsurge of life, and it seemed that the spiritual activity which had extended so rapidly would spread to involve our whole country.

But the Lord leads his Church along other paths: he who had himself drunk the cup of death now offered to his Church the purifying agony of the Cross. And it is in this way that the Church is now climbing Golgotha, spat upon, beaten, derided, and is being stripped and nailed upon the cross. To her faithful children the way is now open for a declaration of faith, for martyrdom, and in particular for much suffering and privation.

Hermit monks once asked the Abba Ischyrion, "What have we achieved?" And he answered, "We have kept the

Lord's commandments." Then they asked further, "What will they achieve who come immediately after us?" He answered, "The life they will lead will be only half as devout as ours." The Fathers asked again, "And those who follow them?" The Abba answered, "They will not lead the monastic life at all, but disaster will strike them, and afflicted by misfortune and temptation they will stand above us and our fathers."

Much suffering and unforeseen attack is the fate of us today. Our existence must be centred in repentance and resistance to temptation. The loss of the external side of Christianity is the greatest of all miseries, and exile, imprisonment and forced labour are nothing in comparison. God's word would indicate that the closure of the churches could have been avoided by repentance: "Turn ye unto me with all your heart, and with fasting, and with weeping, and turn unto the Lord your God: for he is gracious and full of compassion, slow to anger, and plenteous in mercy, and repenteth him of the evil. Who knoweth whether he will not turn and repent, and leave a blessing behind him, even a meal offering and a drink offering unto the Lord your God?" (Joel 2:12-14). Yet when was there ever a general call to repentance? Where did we ever see bishops and priests weeping "between the porch and the altar" and praying for their people? (Joel 2:17).

The diplomatic talents of the bishops were considered of greater value than the word of God; it was on these that man fastened his hopes and in these that he sought salvation. We tried to save the kingdom of truth with a lie.

But the Lord derides that, he pours his scorn upon it all. Joy and gladness have been "cut off before our eyes . . .

and taken from the house of our God" (Joel 1:16). The visible Church is being weakened to the uttermost and deprived of its powers.

My children, God's judgement is now being enforced. We must repent, fall down before God and find the strength to say with the prophets, "I will bear the indignation of the Lord, because I have sinned against him; until he plead my cause, and execute judgement for me: he will bring me forth to the light, and I shall behold his righteousness (Micah 7:9).

The Lord calls us to a new form of salvation. For centuries many churches stood open which had been built and devoutly decorated by human hand. But at the same time there were others not created by man which had remained ignominiously empty and closed. Today the visible churches are being destroyed, but in the grief of penitence there are others arising which have been created by God's hand. The flames of humble martyrdom are flickering about us, particularly in the remoter areas. Starving, ragged, shivering with cold, isolated from the world, on the naked earth, in the snow, or in simple huts, priests and monks and the faithful laity are dying without priestly support and are being refused a grave. In the churches of penitence in their vanishing souls they lift up their prayers for the sins of a Church which had preferred the external to the inner life and was unrepentant even in the face of exceptional suffering.

The light of steady religious commitment is flaming everywhere, from the frozen sea to the scorched desert. With tears of remorse the people, hounded from their churches, continue their praying, and by enduring persecution they are opening up churches in their hearts. Let us too, my dear ones, step into the chambers of the mind, let us enter the temple of our soul, which from its baptism has been dedicated to the Lord and sanctified by him since the first communion. This temple is ours: no one has the power to destroy it except ourselves. Its altar is our heart, and on it we can offer with our tears our great sacrament of repentance. We who have neglected our invisible temple and who have lived off the visible Church will find it hard to accept this new path to salvation laid down for us by the Lord. We shall weep and lament, not with tears of despair but with tears of remorse, and will learn to acknowledge it all as what we deserve. Is it not the Lord who has sent us this? Have not the best of us been treading this path for some time already? For a time or perhaps forever – only God knows – the visible side of Christianity will remain hidden from us.

"Let us stand in reverence as it is meet and right for us to do." Oh for our small and trusted house of God: you granted us such heavenly joy: you were our earthly Jerusalem, our heavenly Zion! "If I forget thee, O Jerusalem, let my right hand forget her cunning. Let my tongue cleave to the roof of my mouth, if I remember thee not, I prefer not Jerusalem above my chief joy" (Ps. 137:5-6).

The Lord has given us a keen sense for spiritual things. Your hearts did not lead you to a place of worship where the divine service entices through splendour, where choice melodies resound and elaborate sermons are held. Our modest small church attracted each of you because you found in it the true way, the way the Church Fathers had ordained. In the brief spring of the Russian Church you were workers in your vineyard. With what self-sacrifice you gave your youth, your maturer years, and the energy of your old age to the construction of the living church of our family of penitents!

You are not merely living witnesses, but are also participating in the final flickering of the lamp of the Russian Church, which the will of God causes to be extinguished.

In the terrible trials to come in the Church of Christ I pray to the Lord, to his most pure Mother and also to our saints that they acknowledge you as true workers in the vineyard of Christ.

My loved ones, let us show ourselves in everything as the servants of God, "in much patience, in afflictions, in necessities, in distresses, in stripes, in imprisonments, in tumults, in labours, in watchings, in tastings" (2 Cor. 6:4-5). And the God of patience and of consolation grant that you live in harmony with one another.

"Become a shrine and a living icon yourself"

Bishop German (Ryashentsev)
Letters to Vera and Natalia V.

Foreword by Natalia V.

The rich spirituality and great religious vigour which I was privileged to experience in the many months of my correspondence with Bishop German gave tremendous support to my faith. His letters were a joy which helped mitigate the terrible pain felt at the sufferings of his endless path of the Cross. They are filled with loving sympathy for the reader's awareness of his situation, an awareness which could only be cautiously and delicately expressed. How gently and sensitively he comes to the aid of a bewildered friend, and it is with such loving forebearance that he recognises spiritual weakness and lack of forcefulness. He is so attentive in his role as father, and so strong in his determination to help and to cure open spiritual wounds. In one of his last letters he wrote, "In drawing nearer to the Lord we also draw near to those around us: neither in life nor in death will anyone ever succeed in destroying our unity." This unity is manifest in its full entirety when he hurries yet again to our aid with the gracious healing power of his living word and in the example given us by his saintly life.

Never did this bishop of God stray even one iota from the path that he had chosen. Calmly he describes his experiences, and with a gentle humour which veils the extent of his suffering. Through this we see his unshakeable religious strength, and how he progresses steadily in his own spiritual development. He never spared himself in anything, but tirelessly and fearlessly gave back to the Lord and to his people the talents which had been granted him, the talents of a witness, a pastor and a singer praising God.

The letters reproduced here cover the following periods of the Bishop's life: his first banishment to the north in 1923, the autumn of 1925 in Volokolamsk, his second banishment to central Asia from 17 November 1925 until the spring of 1928, his appointment that summer in Vyasniki, then fresh arrest in the August of that year, his voyage to Solovki and exile first in Derevansk and Votch, then in Arsamas where he stayed from March 1933 to the spring of 1934, and then in Siberia where he remained until his final disappearance in 1937.

Letters to Natalia

Tobolsk
12 September (NS) 1923

Many thanks for the note you sent to Tobolsk. We have been in Siberia since the 18th, and it welcomed us with wonderful weather which has lasted until today. You know how I love to see the broad fields and forest and water. You can imagine my great delight in encountering people again after the deprivations of the last year and a half, and also in being in contact with nature, taking in the sublimity of her soul and her soothing beauty. After the murky Moscow weather we have been thrilled by the splendid Siberian autumn and it makes us hope that our tribulations might be coming to an end.

Although our place of exile is in the Tyumeny Province and in Tobolsk the people in exile are generally allowed free, I still find myself in the "House of Correction", as the prison here is called. So here is our opportunity to study the Tobolsk version. Our treatment by the authorities is excellent, but it is strange that because there have been no political prisoners here for some time we are often given the same treatment as the criminals. As you know, even in the last administration the treatment of political prisoners – and even more so those like us who have been banned administratively, that is, without the trial to which every citizen has a right – was totally different from the treatment of criminal prisoners. Yet here they want to have as little to do with us as possible, and are so absurd as to put us under guard at times when we should only be supervised. Obviously nobody has begun to consider this strange injustice, or perhaps they are simply apprehensive that ignorance of the regulations might allow them to infringe them. All this focuses attention on us against our will, and results in demonstrations of sympathy from people quite unknown to us. This happens particularly when we are accompanied by a "guard of honour". It happened in Tyumeny, and it is now happening here: attention is thus drawn to us, and then the authorities are astonished that the people know that certain exiles are housed nearby and are surprised when total strangers attend to us as if we were their close relations. I cannot help linking this particular concern for our welfare with

St John of Tobolsk, whose small icon — I no longer remember when and from whom I received it — has accompanied me everywhere for the last two years. It is such a mighty coincidence!

We shall live in the village of Samarovo, in the Tobolsk region, in the province of Tomsk. It is an industrial patch of land 500 kilometres north of Tobolsk on the river Irtysh, and 500 kilometres south of Berysov. To judge from Tobolsk, where we can see melons, water melons and tomatoes growing, it will probably be no colder than at Vologda. Samarovo lies on the steep slopes of the river Irtysh and everyone is unanimous in saying that it is an attractive and healthy area surrounded by pine forest and rich fishing grounds. It seems to me that in general the people in Siberia are by nature more open than our people, and more sympathetic to the needs of others. We think that Samarovo will not add to our sufferings, although naturally a lot will depend upon the nature of our surveillance. But as you know I have nothing to hide and nothing to fear, for my convictions are not concerned with politics but with the realm of conscience declared by Soviet law to be free.

At the moment impressions are flooding in so fast that I am unaware that my friends are far away. In fact it seems just the opposite. And yet it is a shame that again when I left Moscow my ill luck followed me and I was unable to see the people closest to me. What a misfortune, not to be able to bid goodbye to those dearest to you! In this way I lost both my grandmothers, and then both my Mama and Father A(lexander) M(etchov) died recently without my being there. I think that it probably has to be this way if I am to continue to devote my whole life to the truth and to place it before everything else, and if I am to be courageous when for its sake I have to suffer misfortune. And yet: how Massya[1] would like to feel the plush of the divan from time to time! We are waiting for the ship to Samarovo which they say will not arrive before the 5 or 8 September. Please greet your Mama,[2] Father Alexei and all our friends. Pray that the Lord will be always with me. Christ protect you also.

11 October (NS) 1923

The birds have already gathered and flown away. The last ships are leaving, and with them a chain of goods barges, on their way down to the south. Although the warm autumn is much the same here as it is in Sergievo,[3] everything is preparing for its encounter with winter, which in October is already fairly well established. I already have the necessary equipment: high and rather elegant shoes made of fine deerskin with fur both in and out, fur boots, and a fur cap with ear and neck flaps. All these are the results of Tanya's inexhaustible energy and effort on my behalf.[4] What an act of God's mercy to have prompted her to undertake such a courageous task which involves such toil and effort! It could easily have been someone else who had decided to accompany me, but here it is not only good will which is needed but also strong hands and nerves. Our Abbess will soon, I hope, have toughened us up even more. This mean old crosspatch, who reckons she knows everything, and is perfectly content with her own piety (she does not like going to church and criticises those who do) not only lectures Tanya but also me. How that sharpens up my weak patience and even more my deficient humility! I console Tanya by telling her it is the Lord who has sent us such a good instructor as we might otherwise have spent our exile without benefit to our souls. But if only this Abbess did not control our household, if only she was not a trouble-maker. One moment she is filled with emotion because vespers is celebrated regularly in her house and hence we are praying for this "worthy house and all its occupants", and the next she is saying we are filling the whole house with soot from the censer. She worries about every old cast-iron pot and every little piece of string. Yesterday she even took the curtains down from my windows for fear that they could somehow catch fire, and when Tanya remarked that the room was not very nice without them she declared that if I had not been there she would have cleared all the furniture out long ago. Yet this does not prevent her from giving us milk, for instance, when we have none, and from peaceably planning our food and drink with Tanya.

We live in such tremendous isolation that the nearby village of 880 inhabitants impinges very little upon our lives, and we can devote ourselves to religious matters without any particular distraction. I very much regret that despite a certain aptitude I never learned to draw or paint, for this would be very useful to me now in my leisure time. The dough here is too crumbly for making small icons as I did in Butyrki (the Moscow prison). There is a lot that would interest a painter here, and I have captured some of the views in pencil sketches, although they are really only caricatures. Recently the time has been spent on extensive walks and in making a crosier. For the feast of Our Lady's Protection and Intercession (14 October) we have some two- and three-armed lamps of indifferent quality, as well as the crosier made by me, and a mitre put together by both Tanya and myself following an idea of mine. Everything is very simple, but not without a certain elegance.

The so-called faithful here show a marked indifference to church. You can see that from the Abbess herself, who considers herself a pillar of faith, although her intelligence and her knowledge of God's word cannot be denied. But at the same time the people like to order requiem masses for the dead on their name days (to which however they do not come themselves). Some bring their children to communion, and they do in fact help the new arrivals. Although they are very casual in their relationships with one another they are all quite good-natured people. Neither the feast of Our Lady's Protection and Intercession nor the liturgy of a strange bishop have made the slightest impression on them. Except for two small boys no one is allowed in the altar room. The boys are all members of the Komsomol.[5] The brutalising effect of a lack of faith is particularly noticeable in the women, who all smoke, cut their hair short, swear all the time, and nibble at pine kernels the whole day long like squirrels. But this does not prevent them from dressing well and tastefully and in being very keen on neatness at home (though this has less to do with cleanliness than with social aspiration). However none of the houses has a separate toilet, not even an unheated one.

We have been here a month now. As a result of Tanya's efforts I am hardly lacking in anything. Money here has no value at all. The most important item is butter. Now that winter is imminent the drivers will be taking the grain into Tobolsk, and so we shall be able to get what we need through our friends. Thank God we are already surrounded by good people who help us out with petrol and also with other things if necessary. In short, as long as the soul finds its consolation in the divine the rest is either a bonus, or not having it will not oppress the soul. How pleased I am that we can spend our time here in constant religious activity and prayer. So long as I do not have to waste my energy on trivialities. I would so much like to find the time to strengthen true love, true piety and true humility within me. Much which I already had in short supply has become even scarcer in me here. My nerves also need some peace: any small source of agitation and I immediately feel exhausted.

Please share this letter with Vera. I am pleased to hear that she has written not only to myself but also to Sinaida Michailovna, who has at last found herself as a job as a doctor on the railways. The Lord be with her. It is time that she too lost that bitterness with which God wishes to make her soul and actions fully Christian. Pass on my very good wishes to Mama and Slava.[6] I ask for the prayers of the holy startsy. Write to me by registered post and tell me all the news, particularly that which most concerns us both. Greet Vanya[7] and his brothers. On the day of St Sergius I celebrated the liturgy.

4 February (NS)
If it gave you pleasure, my dear Natasha, to prepare the small parcel I have received from you, how can I thank you for the pleasure which through your love I was privileged to experience today in receiving it? From small fragments you have produced a picture of him who is love, and the piece which Father Diomid has added has bestowed upon this hand-created picture a divine splendour which imbues the whole of your parcel with a heaven-sent force.

For me the whole of today has been something special.

I was aware that a postman I knew was due to be buried. He has left behind a wife and three small children who have practically no means of support at all. Whether from a lack of prudence on the part of his relations or for other reasons the dead man almost received no burial service. The priest here was away on pastoral duties, the other one had not been informed and had eaten. I myself had not eaten, so in the Lord's name I decided to consider the strict regulations concerning the celebrant to be less important than love for the soul of the deceased. As we followed the body I read the order of prayer and before the service I cleansed my soul through confession. My God, it did my soul such good! Then the priest read the burial service while I, with a boy and without any vestments, sang the choral parts. We celebrated the funeral rites in their full moving beauty, and to the local people it was as if they were seeing it all for the first time.

I was expecting some parcels today, so when I arrived home I sent Tanya to collect the post. She brought me just your registered letter, and said that no parcels had arrived. But this did not sadden me, for your letter in itself gave me such pleasure as I read of the devotion with which friends and others who do not know me had brought tokens of their love for the Lord to be included in your small box. A little later – quite unexpectedly as is always the way with everything which is divine – people arrived from the post office to notify me not only about one packet but about several from you. The rest you can imagine, even that which took place in my surging heart as I saw before me all these eloquent witnesses to God's unutterable goodness. The best bit I did not find immediately. What grace God has bestowed upon me! Why does he spoil me so? Why am I given these pure white candles, whose flames have always proclaimed the stars to me since my childhood, telling me of heaven and of the angels, of the gentle saints and the light they had kindled in the world, and what they had used to show the way in a world so darkened by the tempter? Why am I given these garments of such purity and softness when it is precisely these attributes which I so lack, although my soul constantly longs for them? Why do I receive this love which has even softened the hearts of those who know more about my errors than about the state of my heart, a heart whose depths have only been plumbed by God? I bow down – literally – to the ground before you all, and praise you in the name of him who, when times allow it, lets people be moved to pity for someone perhaps not worthy at all, so that his soul may be filled with the divine echo of the future life and the eternal. The path which leads to it is arduous, and it is only the tormented who pursue it; but each one of us is expecting that after a life of tears and patience we shall experience immortal joy, a premonition of which is the only thing which gives us the strength to forget the agitation and sorrow of this earthly life. When people who really do not have the time to think much about others go so far as to bestow such love upon such an idle one as I, as you have all done and continue to do, then surely the Lord, as eternal love, is urging us by this means to live in a state of constant repentance so that we might be worthy of his love and the martyr's crown. If there is no gentleness and purity, nor compassionate love, particularly for those who now carry the heavy cross of grief and care for the bride of Christ, and who do not always take the path which is most direct, then even the formal pledge to truth can deprive people of the joy of seeing the Lord in his kingdom . . .

As for me, you know I possess a lot and also very little: a lot has been given me, and I have done very little for it. Once again I ask you, Natasha, to thank the dear starets for me, and also Father Leonid, through whom I always received the grace of St Sergius, as well as my fellow sufferers from the "summer holiday" in Butyrki, Father Potapy,[8] Nad. Al and Nina with Katya, and all who remember me and pray for me.

As a complement to your parcel, so to speak, another one arrived from Danilov:[9] incense, candles and an altar cloth. This is indeed a joy for me, but it is also an injunction to remain true to the Lord not only in what is visible but also in the most hidden dictates of the soul, where in fact our future is written. A little earlier I had received your normal letter, which had crossed with mine. I have written to you and Vanya at No. 7, Dvoryanskaya Street. By now you will probably have received the letter.

I am in good health, thank God, and the weather here is marvellous. The few days we have had without sun and the nights without stars can be counted on the fingers of my two hands. The days are already two hours longer now. We have become accustomed to the cold. Temperatures of twenty degrees of frost are more tolerable than the five to ten degrees of our home town. I mean it.

God protect you. Peace be with you all.

5 April (NS)

Near the corner of my room there is a telegraph pole where the lines from B.S. and Tobolsk meet (the post office is just opposite). Sometimes and especially at night it seems as if it is buzzing with the burden of a profound and endless line of thought; it moans and groans, sometimes echoing as powerfully as the distant sound of bells from countless familiar churches. I often feel it reflects the state of my soul, which is heavy with the melancholy thought that beauty of spirit and truth is fast fading from the world and from our hearts. Much more rarely do I discern in it the transition to those bright sounds from which joy and jubilation arise. Indeed the whole of this middle week of fasting, with its soft sad song of the Cross, and in the evening its hesitant acclaim of the day which will take us beyond trouble, anxiety of mind and passion, all this reminds me of the interchange between light and shade. This is bound to play a part in the life of this world and of ourselves: light and dark, good and evil merge into one another, become intensified, and he who can distinguish between the genuinely good, which represents life, and what is evil and represents death, is particularly blessed. Even happier is he who can remain true all his life and through all swings of mood to what he knows to be right, as is also the one who makes his heart into a shining altar of eternal light and of the eternal word. How lucky we are to have the infinite joy of sharing even in small degree in those wounds by which all mankind has been healed, and to be even a small particle of that eternal force which has shown all creation the way, by a path both eternally old and eternally new, which leads us to the resurrection through renunciation of the self and through love.

Many people consider the quest for the lost paradise, which is an agony usually expressed through a restless search for constantly new ways of life far removed from the way of Christ, to be what life is really all about. A painful obsession with the creation, the desire to use it as the tool for personal pleasure and for homage to the self, is for them the true pulse of life. Yet both the old heathen age and the new have shown and are still quite clearly showing that this is a heavier burden to bear than the yoke of salvation, and a heavier cross than the holy Cross of Christ. And neverthless: how little we avail ourselves of this saving knowledge, how unfaithful we are to that sabbath which brings symmetry to our daily lives and the struggle for existence, and which is then transformed into the joyful celebration of the resurrection! Yet the Lord of that day is the power which triumphs over all the world: this power is revealed through the weak. This I find consoling and improving and it fills me with absolute certainty that on that future day of resurrection we shall all share in the divine jubilation of the kingdom of Christ.

Tomorrow, apparently, the final post leaves. Until June of the new calendar we are likely to be cut off from the world. So I send you greetings for the Easter celebration in advance. God protect you. Pass on my greetings to the startsy, Vanya, Kronya, Potapy, Krotky,[10] and N.A., the Bethanians, those at Gethsemane, and all acquaintances. I suppose you received the registered letter with the water-colour? Very good wishes to Vera and the Ilyinskis.

Christ be with you.

Day of the martyrs Adrian and Natalia
8 September (NS) 1924

My very dear friend Natashenka! With most especial love and sincerity I send you good wishes for your name-day. Today it was somehow easier and pleasanter than usual to pray at the altar for you and your soul which so clearly reflects the bright points of light in this world. As I heard the song of praise for the two Martyrs which emphasises the – if one may say so – unusual religious activity and profound influence of Natalia on Adrian, I involuntarily thought of you. As you know I feel it is no accident that each of us bears the name of a particular saint. God entrusts our soul to precisely that saint who possessed the same virtues and Christian attributes that we are first given, and who built on them and perfected them. And so I feel quite clearly that the work of the Martyr Natalia is now continued through you, and her influence thus extends to more men than merely Adrian.

You know of course that as we go our way many of us encounter much feminine influence, yet very few of us meet with the deep, refreshing and purifying influence of the sort conveyed by the Martyr Natalia and as I have with you. Such a saintly and unclouded friendship, such youthfulness between people who are no longer young, all emphasises for me yet again the truth of those words which state that there is only one victory which the world with its desires, pride and sensuality is able to claim: our faith and its author and perfecter, our master and our Lord.

A snowstorm is raging outside my window. The roofs, trees and earth are coated in white. But my soul expands with warmth and joy when I think of you and experience that mood which I rarely observe in other people, and even in myself.

Today I also remember my other acquaintances who bear the names Natalia and Adrian. In Sergievo there were three others beside yourself. There is also my great admirer and advocate of '22 and '23 when I was ill, Adrian Vifansky, a farmer. In short, today is the day of some very dear namesakes, and is particularly glorious because of Natasha.

Today and tomorrow we are expecting the mailboat from Tobolsk. Someone will go there at the end of the week. It is also possible that another one will arrive as well, so that we might still be receiving post at the end of September. In October there will doubtless be a break. It seems to me that October also brings the winter. We are in good health and doing well. I have not received anything from Pskov for over a month. It causes me some concern.

Please give the small icon to Verotchka.

30 May (NS) 1925

My dear Natasha! Only now am I able to answer your letter of the week of the Veneration of the Holy Cross, although I am not sure when or if you will ever receive this. Your letter is full of sad self-accusation; this means not so much a loss of spiritual energy as extreme physical exhaustion. We, you and I, have not yet reached that spiritual condition where the pure energy of the spirit, or rather, of grace, not only overcomes the weakness of the flesh but also inspires our spiritual life, which is weak and crippled without the help of God. For a time, as long as those physical and mental reserves given us by nature and our parents hold out, the spirit of God and the Lord works through this bodily health and spiritual energy. During this period life does not show us its full face. This is why we are so cheerful and filled with such valuable ideals and other enthusiasms. But sooner or later this phase comes to an end, and for all of us Gethsemane begins, bringing battles and extreme physical exhaustion. Both of these are painful and emotional for precisely the reason that our spirit must be freed of its self-righteousness, however pure and ideal it may seem to us, and must reconcile itself to

God's just will. But God's will restricts our souls and is hard to endure.

Making this transition to the will of God is always painful, as is every transition from a simple to a more perfect and higher form, and every physical and – even more so – every spiritual birth. Here on earth all that we experience is the beginning of this complete rebirth of our will into the will of God, of our understanding – even that of believers – into the divine understanding, and of our inferior and imperfect love into the perfect and all-embracing love of the Holy Trinity. If a person is firmly on the side of this truth, or on the other hand rejects it completely, then he no longer lives but dies, for he has then done everything he can in this life and is ready for the next one.

The purpose of our personal Gethsemane is to fulfil in trembling and in sorrow what is commanded of us, and not to allow ourselves to be distracted by the thought: why is it this way and not otherwise? It takes the form it does because a strong emotional shock dealt us by first-hand experience of good can just as effectively lead us to God as some terrible misfortune. Judas was with Christ the whole time and betrayed him; the thief on the cross had lived his whole life without Christ yet believed him.

If there were not such clear indications of this inter-change between light and dark and of the final triumph of light, both in the life of the Lord and also in the development of our own faith, then life would indeed be terrible. But we should take heart from the words of St Paul, intended for the Jews but also directed at us alive today: "For God hath shut up all unto disobedience, that he might have mercy upon all" (Rom. 11:32).

We do not know how near or how far ahead our fate

will lie, but there is always a time when great emotional turmoil is needed not only to cause us to reflect but also to lead us back to the focal point of all that is truly human: to our hearts. It is this which accounts for your physical and mental exhaustion. Let us carry his Cross submissively, and let us – even if it is beyond this life – look forward to peace from the Lord, and the complete revelation of the hidden meaning of everything which is at present causing us pain and which smites and wounds us.

We are in good health and good heart. The Easter celebrations were enjoyed here with inner delight, yet I fear there are further trials ahead. It would be terrible if this were to lessen our future joy. Praise be to God for all things. Here the rivers are overflowing their banks as usual, but the warm weather has not yet arrived. The ice on the Ob only broke on Ascension Day. I do not know when we shall next have contact with the outer world. Very good wishes to Vera Timofeyevna, the startsy, Vanya and all other acquaintances. Pray that God's will favours us at Whitsun time. Tanya is in good health and kisses you both. I will send you my good wishes for the feast in my prayers. Peace be with you.

Massya's business trip ends on 13 July of the church calendar.[11] Peter and Paul was the last day and Whitsun the first . . . but of what?

Letters to Vera

22 June (NS) 1925

I received your Easter letter, dear Vera Timofeyevna, at Whitsun. From its first to its last line I welcome it as a decorated Easter egg: "Give thanks for what you receive, and do not question."

I totally share your opinion that many of the things with which we – and I most particularly – torment ourselves unnecessarily and which cause us suffering and bring us little salvation arise because none of us can forget that line, "O forest, O life, O sunshine, O happiness and tears", etc., and we weep over the sawdust when we should be asking ourselves how we can use it to build what was previously built from trees. It also serves us right that the air is no longer filled with the perfume of roses but with the rank smell of dirty dish-water, and that strange growths of nettle, burdock and touch-me-not balsam abound. But now that it has happened there is no point in hanging one's head and regretting the absence of fresh roses, but much better to consider how we can contain the smell of dirty dish-water. Also it would be good to know what to wear when our path through life does not take us through a rich meadow of fragrant luscious grass but through a dense and rampant undergrowth of burdock and nettle.

Naturally each Christian must persuade himself of the logic of the position which his faith has placed him in: there are fewer churches, so be one yourself. Also become a temple of God. Entry to many shrines has become difficult, so become a shrine and a living icon yourself. Much of the external apparatus, a lot which the faith of men, women and children depended on at a simple level has disappeared, so give them something of incomparably better standing and which is as obvious to wise men as it is to a child: the simplicity and intensity of devout humility.

It is only our spiritual stagnation which is preventing us from seeing what is happening today as a call for the strengthening of the self, and for self-knowledge and self-denial. As it says in one of our fasting prayers, now "the time for spiritual activity has dawned". In me I feel there is little self-pity; but on the other hand it makes me sad that we use the time allotted to us more for the mind and body than for the spirit. And I love you and the reason why I value your spiritual friendship so much is because I know that in life we need a corrective influence on our different moods, attitudes and activities. You have taken over this indispensable though often boring and thankless task. It is all the more valuable to me in that I — apart from Fedya[12] and Vitya[13] — have no friends who take me to task so often without hurting me and who do not induce a state of stupor in me but keep me on my toes by speaking frankly to me. I know plenty of gentle and soft-hearted people, but they hardly ever tell me what is unacceptable in me, or they talk highly tactfully of a cold when it is a bad case of the flu with complications.

My present seclusion and especially the pleasure of the holy altar, which is decorated just now with beech twigs which I brought on to bud in my room (for the forest is still leafless), so fills my soul that I can almost believe myself to be where Kronya and since last year Father Michey[14] are now living.

As far as grandfather[15] is concerned I have long been of your opinion, although Fedya thought otherwise. It is only to our clever-clever pseudo-brothers that his death has no meaning nor the powerful and sincere love which has been shown him, for they assume that an act of God can be accomplished without God. One of our sacred hymns calls death "the source of our salvation". It is a pilgrimage to the newly discovered relics of a servant of God, and burial is more like restoring these relics to their home again. This is such a pleasant and consoling sign from God that I feel not the slightest unease or despondency about this death. Obviously everything was done which had to be done, and now it is better that someone else should continue the work.

For myself all I wish is the one thing: really to be what I must be. I take everything which is now happening to be such a great act of mercy from God that I fear more and more that the Lord could be granting me such consolation on this earth for my good intentions that in the next life I can expect to be most terribly dispossessed: so much has been given me and such a small percentage of benefit has accrued.

We are in good health, thank God, and in good heart. It is getting warmer. God protect you. Pray for us.

Chodshely
Karakalpakish
Kazakhstan
5 December (NS) 1926

Tomorrow, my dear Vera Timofeyevna, is the feast of St Mitrofan, your favourite feast-day.[16] The Lord having granted you such a generous degree of quick temper and firm character, you love everything which is calm and gentle and innocent. Nobody yet knows for what purpose more effort of will is needed, whether for what is normally called practical activity, or for those seemingly passive virtues which so marked the Bishop of Voronezh.

Since our separation I do not believe I have received anything in writing from you. Of course I cannot really demand it, for I know that you are now accomplishing a great act of faith, which is to live the penitential life at a time when it is physically and spiritually difficult, and in your opinion could even be pointless. Nevertheless I would now and then like to glimpse the state of your soul, even if it is "only" by means of letters. As long as your hand can still hold a pen you should not deny it to yourself and others.

I have already told you often about my daily life here. At the moment I am distressed that my registered and air letters and indeed even my telegrams might not be reaching their destination. This time a wall has been erected between me and my distant friends. Last time I felt so closely linked to you, but this time I feel just as strongly that I am either retreating from you, becoming insensitive and cold and withdrawing spiritually, or that the Lord is allowing me to experience a level of misery I have not yet known, and is teaching me to accept my helplessness. In the first month of our life here I was receiving no answer from anywhere – not even from Moscow – to my letters and telegrams concerning the danger of my situation, and I was overcome by the frightening feeling of being outcast and estranged from the people closest to us. It was not rational thought, but dreary and pathetic shreds of worthless and endless fantasy; it was not prayer, but the pitiful and vain flickering of once brightly flaming spiritual torches. There was neither the quiet courage of patience in it, nor any great hope that the Lord – despite all the obstacles we erect along the path to ourselves – would hear and come to my aid in time. In every single thing without exception, in my daily life, in outward things (but essentials), and – even more – in the hidden corners of my heart, in everything there was such a terrible void that even without any pride there would have been a danger of sinking into despair.

After the feast of the icon of Our Lady, "The joy of all that mourn", there was a change for the better for us all. A room was found for me. It is true that money was extorted from us for getting it into good order, and what is more with impossible conditions: we were obliged to pay four months in advance. But by the sixth month we had more or less settled down and an altar had been erected for us all in my room, and then naturally our sufferings were halved. I say halved, for I am quite unable to link the spiritual life with matters of daily existence. In fact the business of procuring food, cleaning, finding firewood and water, washing and other trivialities do not take up much time. It is not the lost time, but much more a certain inner protest against these things. I console myself with thinking that when Chrysostom was in exile even he wrote in his letters of the physical inconveniences. It is clear to me that tiredness does not stem from the work itself but much more from an awareness that time is passing so prosaically. So I really appreciate it when there is no washing-up to be done, when prepared meals will last for two or even three days, and it is possible to live in surroundings which to some degree are clean. Only once have I taken pencil to paper. Although I am living in a much frequented place, thank God in my room it is quiet. When I light the lamp it becomes warm and cosy, and there are five of us, two bishops, an archpriest and two nuns, who gather together in his name. How terrible it would be if this joy did not exist.

God willing, this letter will reach you before the feast-days. I greet you lovingly. Pass on my prayer greeting to all startsy who are near or in the wilderness. Let them mourn those who may well be bearing the burden of misfortune for more than merely their own weakness; and if they still contain some small spark of prayer then we would like to receive it, so that our prayers may become deeper too. Greet everyone who took part in the harmonious discussions we had at your house. The Lord and Holy Virgin protect you all.

Letter to Natalia

Feast of the Centurion Longinus
29 October (NS) 1928

Please do not be upset, my dear Natasha, if I am late with this answer to your letter about your problems of enforced separation, estrangement and egoism. In your letter you promised "to continue in a few days's time", and so I waited. But in the meanwhile a letter from Lelya has arrived, and with no sign of your sequel. Perhaps you have reconsidered it and no longer want to write about something you find so important and delicate. The last thing I want to do in this letter is to comply with the old saying, "Other peoples' sorrows are easy to bear", but I must confess I feel a certain helplessness. I will not hide from you that when I learned of some of the background to your leaving Sergievo I involuntarily let slip the question, "But why did she do that?" The pain which you described to me, that suffering which undermined your resolve and reduced you to despair, explains to some extent why you did it. Your actions revealed a strong love for your mother as well as self-denial and self-sacrifice, yet also, it seemed to me then, a lack of reflection. If such a step had been necessary you, as well as others, would have been asked to do it by your Mama. But no one asked you: you did it all on your own. You have taken upon yourself a cross which perhaps was not intended for you at all, so now far from feeling the pleasure of a task well done before God and your fellow beings and a surge of spiritual energy and vitality, you are now demoralised, filled with spiritual apathy and the desire to forget yourself.

Seen from the sidelines it seems as if you had exhausted all your rich store of love for your mother in a way that did not actually bring the benefit to her which in your state of despair you had hoped. Then when you were asked for material assistance and help for her and for yourself, you were unable to offer either the one or the other. You were completely exhausted by the terrible emotional crisis, which could have been avoided if someone had stopped you in time and prevented you from rushing into this physically debilitating act of heroism; and in this mood you became painfully aware of some of Lelya's weaknesses, indeed they expanded out into whole dark rings, which the light of your own personal happiness had evidently always suppressed in your mind. But now they came to plague you, literally so coldly and mercilessly that you were unable to ignore them.

Now the Lord is giving you the opportunity to test your spiritual strength and to appreciate that wise church ruling which says you should never impose martyrdom upon yourself if you are not called upon to accept it. Why? Because in one's spiritual development it is essential to regulate the advance from virtue to virtue and not to act prematurely, and because if an action which in itself is good is undertaken at the wrong time and with no blessing it will not benefit the soul but may harm it.

Now it could be that not only your Mama but also many other things seem to you otherwise than they really are. The egoism of your Mama, her impulse to cross all your efforts, is simply the "but" of age and experience. It would be monstrous to suppose that it is concern for her personal safety and welfare (even if it is also for the happiness of an only and much-loved daughter). In your present situation you may well feel that you have ruined your life, that you have not attained that happiness that most women do and that you have lived like some sexless being, etc. Evil often exploits such a state of mental tiredness and displays before us the transitory image of a life with other dimensions and with other tempting pleasures, as well as one of comfort bringing peace and relaxation. I reckon that it must have exerted itself quite considerably in this unfortunate business to have worn you down in the battle not only against obstacles it has itself erected in your path, but also in the battle against all-consuming emotions, and to have made you receptive to the idea of a life which would not provide you with the depth of feeling and frame of mind you experience in the religious life without your femininity. The fact is that you would never forgive the betrayal of what has brought you so close to St Sergius and the Hermitage and to many other things in your present life and in the eternal.

The estrangement from Lelya of which you write is nothing more than tiredness and a healthy dose of irritation because you have had to cope with so much on her account which she does not understand, and now she is expecting yet further sacrifices from you. In your present situation you will remember something of a person who cried his eyes out over a book, exhausting all his reserves of tremendous talent and clarity of mind, so that when the real life knocked on his door he suddenly found he no longer had what he had wasted. I by no means want to criticise you, my dear Natasha, I am merely analysing. Yet just like you I am obliged to have recourse to pen and ink to help me, and this does not always accurately express what would be immediately understood without words in a personal conversation. I do not doubt for a moment that everything which you are finding difficult at present will pass and be comprehensible again, and that you will rediscover good and be as fresh and as tireless as ever. Christ protect you.

Postcard to Natalia

4 September (NS) 1931

Perhaps you will receive this card in time to bring you my very good wishes for the feast day St Adrian and St Natalia. I have already written to you from this area: I am in the same situation here as I was in Siberia and in the south. Did you get my postcard? Is Vera Timofeyevna still alive? Where is she, and is she well? As you know I have been at the same place as Lartshik.[17] There I had typhus for two months, as did Father Maximilian whom I found there already, much aged but strong and absolutely untouched in spirit. To the priests there he gave the same support as did Hippolytus, and having him there was very good for my nerves which after my illness and other temptations were rather shattered. I too have aged, and have white hair. You would probably have difficulty recognising me, expecially if you remember me in vestments and rather younger. Yet I have retained a vigilance of spirit, and age has not affected the vitality of those deep feelings which bind me to my small cell at the Holy Trinity Monastery and to its inhabitants.

Since July I have been living in Veliky Ustyug, 2nd

Proletarian Street, No. 6. One can write to my brother Kolya, Victor Stepanovitch Ryashentsev. It would give me such inexpressible pleasure if you would send me one or two words about yourself and your Mama, or at least your address. In this area Kolya experienced much that was difficult to see and endure, but now he is living more or less peacefully. Vitya took over from him a short time ago and has gone to Zossima.[18] Greet your Mama. The Lord be with you.

"Everything lies in God's hand"

Letters from Father Anatoly Shurakovski,
and reminiscences of him

Father Anatoly Shurakovski was born in 1897 of
an educated family and grew up without any
religious instruction. When he was still a student
he was active in the Philosophy of Religion
Society at Kiev, and at twenty he was converted.
In 1915 he was a student at the Kiev Vladimir
University, and in 1920 he was ordained priest.
Through his sermons many young people, particularly from the intelligentsia, collected around
him. In 1923 he was arrested for the first time and
sent into exile. After a year and nine months he
was allowed to return to Kiev. In 1930 he was
arrested again, and was in prison until his death
from tuberculosis on 10 October 1939.

A reminiscence

In 1930 on the Feast of Our Lady's Protection and
Intercession Father Anatoly celebrated the divine service
for the last time. On 1 October he was arrested and held
in Moscow for a long period, first at Lubyanka, then in

Butyrki (two notorious Moscow prisons), and sentence was finally passed on him after a year's inquiry. He and Bishop Dmitry of Gdovsk were called out of their cells to listen to the verdict: "Death by shooting". The priest and the Bishop crossed themselves, then after a few painful seconds the remainder of the verdict was read: the death penalty had been reduced to ten years' camp imprisonment.

So began his journey through the camps – Sviri, Solovki, the White Sea Canal . . .

Letters

Svirilag
December 1931

I am considerably nearer home than I had supposed, being not in the Solovki but in the Sviri camps.[1] My address is: Vashany, Leningrad province, Unit 2, Sviri Camp. I am doing various occasional duties and office work, and most frequently as guard. Guard duty, consisting of eight hours outside on one's own, suits me well, provided I have warm clothes and do not feel the cold. Living conditions have been variable, but at the moment perfectly satisfactory. My health is as normal, and even the food is quite acceptable. I am in good heart and I live in faith in God . . .

Svirilag
14 January 1932

I am receiving letters and parcels. After a redefinition of categories I have been allocated the third invalid category, where allowance is made in the amount of work I do per day. The length of my imprisonment dates from 30 November of the old calendar, which is calculated from the day of my arrival in Moscow. My sentence is based on the sixth or eleventh point in Paragraph 58.[2] My new address: Svirstroy, Leningrad province, Unit 1, Sviri Camp. I am now living in the forest, where it will certainly be pleasant in the summer, and am sharing a room with one other person which for me is unprecedented luxury. I am not working much and am helping out voluntarily with the accounts, as my tuberculosis frees me from any forced labour.

Tolstoy-Datche[3]
18 March 1932

I am now classified by my TB as "chronically sick", and am lying on a special bed of planks in a large wooden hut. This hospital atmosphere is only too familiar to me, for wherever I go I always find myself in a sick-bed. The last time I was in Butyrki I was in the sick bay, and indeed was there twice (. . .) It was odd to to be taken into a room I already knew, for both times I was in the same room as in 1923. Here I am now in the sick bay for the second time, this time for over a month. Yes, it is my usual familiar consumption flaring up again.

In the hut there are a great many people, but I am on my own amongst them. The majority are criminals, with their intolerable jargon and their minds twisted and depraved since childhood. So for days on end I do not say anything, but I often listen. I would like to explore the terrible world of these people and try to understand how they live. My silence and my solitude do not oppress me.

It all reminds me of the unforgettable days of those four months' isolation when I was not only alone but had no books at all.

31 March 1932

Imagine a chemist's shop with all sorts of bottles and a great variety of little glass jars, and a pair of scales, and in the midst of all these I am standing working, dressed in a white overall. The work is interesting, even exciting. In my free time I am studying the theory of pharmacy, and have ordered a range of books on the subject. Living conditions are good, better than at any period of my imprisonment. My health has improved enormously and has returned to normal.

This is my life at present. What will happen tomorrow I do not know, for things change here very frequently.

The caresses which God bestows upon us on our difficult journey give us an idea of the boundless joy and grace which await us in the arms of the Heavenly Father. You will remember how on the Day of the Forty Martyrs we three read the Sticheron together, and the words of St Basil the Great: "Winter is harsh, but paradise is sweet; the frost is agonising, but eternity is blessed." How often in my isolation I have exchanged these words with you in my thoughts, and have remembered the songs and hymns I love so much . . . Here it is spring already. Although no vision of beauty awaits me through the window, when I wake in the morning I can see the sky pink and light blue and everything is gilded by the rays of the sun.

Easter Saturday

On Easter Saturday, at the time when the altar decoration is changed and the priests remove their robes of mourning, I am no longer there at the altar, and I make no change of clothing. I grieve and work, but my soul sheds its sorrow and clothes itself in joy and exultation. Praise be to God, says, no, *sings* every fibre of my whole being: praise be to God!

1 May 1932

I am sitting outside the camp by the high fence. In front of me I can see our northern forests stretching out, with glades and individual clumps of trees in view. The morning is clear and the sky a bright blue. It is seldom like this here, for the sky is usually a leaden grey. My health is in its normal state, and I am no longer working as a chemist but again as a guard (I guard the hay). Again I have long hours on my own. I feel I need it: the soul is free, praying is easier, memories and thoughts intermingle . . . I have received Turayev's *History of the Orient* and am reading it a little. I am living in the general hut and my guard duty is at the camp fence.

31 May 1932

The Lord has deprived me of what is best of all, the altar and my activity as priest. For how long I cannot say, but I know and acknowledge that it is right and just. "Just art thou, O Lord, and righteous are thy judgements." My life continues as usual. We are woken at five o'clock by a terrible din and have to hurry to get to the huts for our porridge. By seven o'clock everything must be done, and then we settle down quickly to work. At present we are working in the forest: tree-trunks are delivered us, and we sort them out and remove the bark. This suits my level of physical fitness and I think that in summer it is healthier than staying indoors. My face has got quite blackened from the rays of even this northern sun, and also from the wind ... I return tired from work, eat about four o'clock (one of our fellow prisoners cooks us something from our own stores which is additional to the general meal), and then I lie down for a couple of hours. After roll call I am usually outside where I can think and remember things on my own and sometimes strike up a conversation. At ten I perform the evening prayers and at eleven or twelve I fall into a good sound sleep. Here the nights are quite white, without shadow or darkness.

So much for the pattern of my external existence. My inner life is quite a different world, one of memories, dreams, hopes, and all that lies beyond our dreams, which is fragments of genuine existence. There is so little external emotional pressure here that the inner world, with its treasures and its questioning, becomes clearer than ever.

During my life I have read and reflected so much. After the word of God my favourite and what I consider to be most essential reading is what I read earlier, regrettably only fleetingly, in the books by religious controversialists. For hours at a time I try to assemble their words in my mind, and when I have found them I encircle them mentally in my thoughts.

"The altar of the heart", "Pray without ceasing", "May the name of Jesus be united with your breath", "Wherever you are and whoever you are with, always be the last", "The greatest and most important thing in life, the science of sciences and the art of arts, is to study and know oneself." For me that is the most essential task of all. I remember St Ignatius.[4] After a long life he wrote on his way to Rome, "I am now finally beginning to become a disciple." How much I would also like to begin to learn inwardly, and after so many oh such scattered years be able to say with him, "I am now beginning to become a disciple." I quite sincerely believe that the miracle would then be achieved, and also the painful but wonderful gift of suffering. Then, if only for a single final time in my life, he might accept the words of the elevation of the host from me as his priest. So be it, so be it.

11 June 1932

... At present a return to the altar seems not only impossible but quite simply inconceivable. "I am not worthy" is always in the forefront of the mind of a priest. And to me it now seems as if I would not risk, like David, even so much as touching the shrine. I would only kiss the earth from afar, from the place where the view opens out over the country of the shrine.

Now I have something to do: I am weaving baskets from great strips of wood. I am surprised that I have any success at all at this strange and unaccustomed craft.

It is already ten o'clock. Night has fallen, a night as light as day, reminiscent of the day when the sun stood still.

Solovki
25 October 1932

The sea, again the sea, commanding, powerful, boundless and majestic. I can see it now as I saw it in those days when we were all so close, those days now gone when we shared such joy and love. Then I see it again, but differently, it does not look the same, it is dark and cold and black . . . and yet it is still the sea. I am enfolded in the protection of him who will lead me on the path which is right. I am content with the move I have just made, and do not regret leaving the boggy Sviri marshland. The living conditions were also not easy there, and I had no particular friends, so there was nothing to lose. Here however I am discovering a beauty of nature which is not only "transparent" but simultaneously splendid and restrained. It is clear why Nesterov once came here to paint.[5] All this is only my first impression, but it is one of great mildness and solemnity. It struck me from the very first moment, when I arrived two days ago with the others late one evening after three hours of pitching and tossing which luckily does not seem to have affected me at all, and set foot on this island and saw before me the walls and towers of the Solovki monastery under a northern starry sky.

My address: Archangel'sk Province, Post Box Popen Island, Unit 1 of the Svirylag, Area no. 1.

21 December 1932

Living conditions are so good here that if this were the start of our period of separation I would propose that you join me. I have been allocated Category 2, and do not do any heavy tasks, remaining at my old work. I believe that nothing terrible can happen here.

I only think of the one thing. They say that in summer many seagulls move in and settle in the Kremlin here, almost as if they were tame. From the top of the Kremlin steps I watch flaming clouds of triumph over a dark and stormy sea. Here life too is a stormy boundless sea, and there on the horizon I can see strong rays of light which never fade. Immortality becomes so clear, so certain and so self-evident, particularly after the single cell.

Solovki
28 March 1933

It is clear why Easter week falls in the spring: its mysterious sense of urgency and sadness of heart is always bound up with the first spring-like blossoming of the soul. And with these happy memories there are others which arise: the church, the divine service and the hymns of Easter week, the series of biblical texts, the wedding feast, the decorated house of God, and his face, so sombre in this period. And although he has robbed me of the joy and wonder of these services I feel that everything I was permitted to experience in and through them is stored up within me, constituting such a tremendous source of riches that my soul could live off it not merely for months but for years or even centuries. Here, just as there in church, his sad and gentle look strikes my heart, which is ashamed and full of the knowledge of its unworthiness. For the joy of resurrection fills the whole world, and is also in us and for us.

Solovki
26 May 1933

Three days ago we finally had some relatively warm days. It smelt of warm wind, and the wind is the decisive factor in the weather here.

The island is transforming itself into a real fairy-tale. The day before yesterday (it was a free day) I walked about at length, clambering from vantage point to vantage point, and from every hill a new fairy-tale opened up, a new poem, one of peace, silence, blue, enclosed. Numerous small lakes are freeing themselves of ice, as if they had been protecting whole sealed-in worlds of a harmony as clear as glass. Everywhere rows of everlastingly fresh pine trees are pushing forwards, pointing upwards. And everywhere is the sea, free and boundless, its surface broken here and there by ice floes driven together by the ocean.

It is so unusual to see the sea and to hear the familiar call of the cuckoo at the same time. The buntings twitter unceasingly and wild geese swish over me with their peculiar noise.

The nights: here the sun has no evening, it does not set. At one or two in the morning I can still read as if it were day. Everything is so strange, just like a fairy-tale.

Solovki
9 August 1933

The roughness of life here, the crudeness of the people round me which extends into real degeneracy, is a great trial. Ugly words, gestures, glances, in short, these moral knocks from my fellow beings are incomparably worse and more harrowing than everything else, than all dirt and darkness or hunger.

The Loving One will lead me to Mount Tabor, that I believe and hope. He robs me of every pleasure, even the joy of prayer. He allows my heart to suffer wounds both deep and small, so that, completely crushed, bleeding, and acknowledging its boundless weakness, it will place itself absolutely and for always in the hands of God. I observe myself with involuntary unease. Deprived of all external help, the death of the soul seems almost unavoidable. Then

I remember his words, "My power is mighty in weakness", and I touch the hem of his garment.

Externally everything is going well. I am now a clerk in the solkhoz. The work is tedious and new for me, but that is unimportant. I am still receiving parcels, and over the summer I have improved in strength. I walk a lot and bring back bilberries and blackberries. I am living in a nice well-lit room behind the Kremlin, and beauty glows in all the windows.

The sea, the lake and the rocks are also beautifully arrayed.

The days race by.

Parandovo
26 Feburary 1934

Sunday of the Veneration of the Holy Cross (the third Sunday of the fast). Tomorrow I am off somewhere, apparently back to camp Section 4. Such is my restless and homeless existence here. Yet I feel that the month I have spent on the banks of the tumbling River Vyg has not raced by in vain, for I have had time to think about many things.

The reasons for the move are unclear. But where we are going is essentially unimportant, as long as my heart remains in him and with him.

Parandovo
27 February 1934

My life is gradually becoming regular again. Now I am a statistician, and living conditions are really good . . . All in all things are not too bad for me in the camp, that is the main thing . . .

Sosnovets
[undated]

I take all trials upon myself. They have already begun. Everything was so good, the work, the people . . . Yet as is usual as I pass through the camps it has all changed at a stroke, and right from the first day. I am now in the general huts doing general duties. But it does not worry me or upset me any more . . . It all happened this way without the slightest reason. Please do not send me anything inessential, for it will be difficult for me to receive goods. My address: Unit 5, BBK (White Sea, Baltic Canal), village of Sosnovets, Camp Section 2.

Vygozero
1 March 1934

I am by the River Vyg again, where I have been put on general duties. I am working outside, sawing and building. It actually seems better and simpler than heavy office work. All in all I feel that these external changes to my life now agitate me less and less, although they naturally exhaust me physically. The problems with the delivery of mail depresses me excessively. I am living in a small hut on the banks of the Vyg. Here there used to be settlements of Old Believers who were seeking to escape the law. The Vyg is a remarkable river: it does not freeze but races endlessly along in its deep stony bed, sometimes gently, sometimes strongly. Its path takes it over steps of stone and here and there it forms waterfalls.

Early in the morning I trudge along the snowy path and look across at the other bank. Every day it is decorated anew and depicts the revelation in gold and purple and blue.

Sosnovets

22 March 1934

Arrived this evening in Sosnovets on account of my TB, together with invalids and other prisoners who have been summoned for a medical check-up. What will come of it I do not know. I fear merely more travelling and moving on. But everything lies in his hands.

Journey went well and am settling in after a fashion. But everyone here is new, I know nobody. Perhaps I shall be going to Kusema with a group of invalids in the ninth unit.

Sosnovets

27 April 1934

So I stayed here after all, and have not been classified as fully invalid (Category 3, 60% light work in the camp). I am pleased to have escaped a long journey with many tedious stages. I have not yet been allocated a definite job but today was sent to do general duties. It is not difficult. How things will develop further I do not know, but it seems I have escaped worse things (Solovky and other alternatives). I have received the parcel. The delivery of mail will be altogether better here, for we have a central distribution centre. Do not send groceries which require cooking, for the stoves are not available in the winter and there is nowhere to cook.

Tunguda
April 1934

I am writing from a new place, Camp Section 2, Unit 5 at Tunguda. Arrived here last night. How long I shall stay I cannot say but I think we shall soon be moving on again. Where to? Perhaps to Solovky, perhaps to another desolate region. I am calm and cheerful. External conditions are good, though parcels have been held up somewhere. It is particularly irritating that the boots have not yet arrived.

Sosnovets
May 1934

I am here doing general duties . . . How good it is to know that everything lies in God's hand, that there is no special work to be done for him and no special place to serve him in, that any work and any place is right. Like this narrow stony path which winds its way through miserable pine trees and bushes which are only now beginning to come into leaf: it is his path. Or the work with trees and planks which we haul out of the wood: it is his work, I am serving him. And even these wooden huts with their slatted beds, they too can be his mysterious kingdom, full of grace.

We now have the facilities to cook again. I am overwhelmed by your boundless and selfless generosity.

Sosnovets
17 May 1934

We are on the road again. In two days I have to go to Tunguda and wait there for the next transfer. My hopes for better living conditions were premature. As for the rest, I do not have much to lose here and I no longer react so sensitively to this moving around and the inconvenience.

The last days were very tedious. For a period I was a statistician again, where the situation required that I work both day and night without break. That was naturally worse than any general duties, for it made me nervous and confused and I was unable to enjoy and spend the beloved days of Whitsun as I wished. Only in occasional moments did joy settle deep in my heart in the midst of all the turmoil and activity, and I thanked God until I was carried along again by the whirl of meaningless industry.

A reminiscence

Tunguda

May 1934

We arrived at the Tunguda camp in the morning. (This was not the first and only visit that Father Anatoly received at this camp. His spiritual children will remember that until 1935 more than one visit a year was allowed. It depended on the prisoner's work and on the judgement of the camp administrators. These visits were granted to relations, although the degree of relationship was un-important and whether it existed or not was not generally checked. The visitor was allowed a certain number of hours, and a number of days in which these hours could be "used up", for instance, sixteen hours would be allowed in eight days, that is, two hours a day. Nevertheless it sometimes happened that the guards were negligent and the visit could be extended. The responsibility for regulating these visits lay with the Head Guard to whom visitors had to show their passports and visiting permits. Members of the parish visited Father Anatoly for the first time in 1932 at Candlemass, then at Christmas 1933, but a third visit scheduled for the Feast of the Icon of Our Lady of Kazan never took place as the prisoner had been moved. At the same time Nina Shurakovski, released from camp, came to Kem only to discover that her husband was not there, and sent a parcel on to him. On her return to Kiev she found a letter of thanks had arrived from him. In 1934, thanks to the leniency of the camp administration, Nina Shurakovski was able to visit her husband, despite the fact that all prisoners had been forbidden visits shortly before. This is the visit described here.)

The Governor of the camp strictly forbade us to see the father, quoting a general decree. On the other hand he permitted us to stay in an empty hut, the so-called "Visitors' Hut", and promised that when work was finished he would send us a prisoner who would take our parcel from us.

Not far from the camp there were excavations in progress. Men in grey jackets, in groups or on their own, were digging or using wheelbarrows. To the side there were armed soldiers standing guard.

We approached the digging. The cold sky of the north was overcast and frosty rain was drizzling down. Everything was grey, ugly and desolate. From time to time a powerful gust of wind blew across, and the blighted birches curved over towards the ground. Our feet sank in the sticky black earth and we found it difficult to move forward. As we came up to the workers we recognised our dear father. He was standing there leaning on a shovel. His thin emaciated face was quite furrowed by the wind and very bronzed. His jacket and his cap were sodden, and clumps of filthy earth caked his shoes. Finally he turned round and saw us . . . He was very hungry and as he ate the bread we had with us a nervous trembling seized him.

But in the evening, after work, the prisoner "ordered to take our parcel" came, and it was none other than Father Anatoly himself.

In the small weakly-lit hut I fed the guard with food I had brought with me. He ate willingly, and entered into conversation. He was in no hurry to leave and paid no attention to his prisoner who sat in a dark corner with his wife Nina. As the parcel she had brought with him was "too large", there was ample excuse to come again the next evening, accompanied by a guard, and to fetch the remainder.

Letters

Nadvoitsy
16 August 1934

I have moved yet again. Yesterday I bid Tunguda goodbye and especially the hut by the dam in which I leave so many memories.

During the night the whole brigade arrived in Nadvoitsy. We covered forty-five kilometres of the route by boat, on the canal and on the Vyg, travelling about twelve hours, and the day was sunny and hot. The few clouds were shot through with light and it penetrated my soul. The air is better here and the earth cleaner than in Tunguda (the earth is not muddy but stony). Everything is correspondingly bright and clear and is reminiscent of Solovky. Lake Vyg is particularly beautiful, shimmering amongst the trees.

Nadvoitsy
19 August 1934

It is already night, and the hut is asleep as I write. What shall I say to my God about today on the Day of Judgement, and about all my previous years? Today, too, he is just to have robbed me of that which I was called to do, which is participation in his Last Supper. Separation from his throne is a constant source of agony to me, yet my heart acknowledges the justice of his judgement.

In the last few days I have not been as cut off from my fellow men as I usually am, and have therefore been unable to collect my thoughts in my "inner cell". But the dissipation of energy and mental distraction sap and wither everything within me. All true pleasure and the whole of life is locked up in our inner store, and if our hearts become impoverished then life becomes trite and stale.

I am working as a woodcutter. The weather is exceptionally beautiful, with clear bright days, although it is getting colder day by day. Soon we shall be needing mittens. I have been sent so many. I await the promised books.

Nadvoitsy
6 September 1934

My life continues to take place at two levels. Externally nothing much has changed: there is a lot of work and tiredness. I have sawn a lot of wood, and am capable of stacking up to ten cubic metres in the time allotted. Now I am shunting earth, using a wheelbarrow and a couple of planks, and despite the tiredness and exhaustion I can feel some benefit from the physical exercise. There is something in it which resists all haste and which harmonises with my mental activity, indeed promotes it. And that is what is most important of all, this "second life", the genuine life, which changes from day to day and must be constantly recreated. Sometimes it seems as if one is just about to reach the longed-for gate to the kingdom of God, as if that difficult prime task in life has been accomplished with a final burst of effort and the point has been reached when the whole world unfolds in bright rays of grace where calm and peace and God are near.

So it seems, but the moment passes, and some accidental circumstance, some irritating triviality or a sudden inner rage will show me how difficult it is to find this path to God, and that everything I was dreaming of is still far away. I constantly feel a learner. It sometimes seems to me that the genuine practical lessons in philosophy are not held in the comfort of a university seminar but at the wheelbarrow. But here I will not be given an examination certificate . . .

Nadvoitsy
4 February 1935

Recently I have been finding the work exceptionally exhausting. I have been working in the woodwork department, which is even more tiring than sawing (although my status as invalid would forbid the latter). I tire quickly, but nevertheless life seems so full and interesting and rich. The first and most important task is that inner one which I constantly have before me: building an inner church. I note how puny my efforts are and am aware that the whole of my life so far has not even been enough to lay the foundations. Tides ebb and flow, and how often the low tide takes me back to my starting-point, at the same time destroying the fruits I had already harvested. But nevertheless how fulfilled I feel by the rotation of the various spiritual tasks and prayers. These are carried over into my physical work, removing its thorns and transforming it invisibly into service. At the same time I see this immersion in myself as service to the world. And when I assemble my long list of names of loved ones, like precious pearls on a rosary, I can feel that the great distance which separates me from them disappears.

The second is the mental stimulation. Even on the most difficult days I manage to read something demanding and to reflect on it. And at the present, when I get back from work at half past five and can rest until seven, I take up a book and as I read and think I am entirely unaware of the noise in the hut. Everything is orientated towards the one centre, and the point which is directed at the foundations of my philosophy of life becomes joyful affirmation within me, a hosanna . . . A few days ago I happened to hear the glorious Moonlight Sonata which I so love.

Now to more prosaic matters. It is not necessary to buy and send me trousers for I have received a good pair of padded ones still in decent condition.

Nadvoitsy
10 May 1935

Somewhere there must be a really warm spring. There must be a place where the birches are now coming into leaf, where daffodils and lilac are in bloom, and where the sun is strong enough to warm you with its golden rays. Yesterday it was already the Spring Feast of St Nicholas.[6] But under our northern sky nobody has yet noticed any change. At best you may feel something spring-like in the

air. Even when over the knitted vest you put a warm shirt
and a pullover and then also a padded jacket you are still
freezing by mid-day, although a little less on those rare
days when there is no north wind blowing. The river has
now darkened and will soon begin to move. It is true that
the snow is only patchy now, but all this is as little like a
true spring as agonising loneliness is like a real and
resonant life full of light and laughter. All I need is patience
. . . as long as the soul does not catch cold in the process,
as long as it does not wither and decay for good in this
rush of activity and crushing lack of joy. And yet I know
that the Lord is near, that this darkness and poverty
of spirit originates in myself and in my own spiritual
joylessness.

Nadvoitsy
27 August 1935

I do a lot of reading, but would give the whole of the
relatively large library here for a shelf of my own books.
Altogether I am becoming more and more convinced that
the classics should be constantly re-read and reconsidered.
This is far more rewarding than any occasional reading.
So I often re-read "Hamlet". For me this book mirrors the
world. The interpretations by Goethe, Byelinsky and Freud
do not seem adequate to me, for in my understanding,
which bases itself on the idea of resurrection and mourning
for the dead father, Hamlet is splendidly intuitive and a
truly human document.

Do not worry about my health. Everything is all right.
I am being given shots of arsenic which does not suit me
very well for it makes me ravenously hungry. I am working
as usual. My "duty" consists of sawing and unloading tree

trunks, often at night which is unpleasant. Soon our woodwork factory will come into service.

Sometimes it seems to me that age could bring that happiness which we seek like a blue bird throughout the course of our lives. To reach a state of calm beyond breathless passion and at the same time preserve the light of a youthful heart and spirit: that is what I am waiting and hoping for.

Nadvoitsy
16 November 1935

I have some news to report. Paragraph 401 of the penal code says that a prisoner can be released from imprisonment early, after having served only half his sentence. This paragraph, although often applied in the prisons, has never yet been adhered to in the camps. But now a decree has arrived whereby this and other paragraphs should be extended to all camp prisoners, whatever the grounds for their conviction and length of sentence. Those who have already completed half their sentence have been told it is possible to write a petition which would be vetted by the commission here and then passed on to a higher authority. So I too, as well as many others, have made my application, but without much hope for success . . .

Nadvoitsy
4 December 1935

When I imagine freedom it looks something like this: a tiny room in some quiet, deserted corner. All access is cut off except for a window which allows the golden rays of the sun and the azure blue of the sky to penetrate. Of the external world only the essentials remain, which is work for one's daily bread, preferably semi-physical, like guard duty. Near the icon there is a reading desk, I open the book and read, following the church cycle, and move from word to word, from spectacle to spectacle, from thought to thought, and from light to the light of God. Of all my memories of a life rich in impressions it is the childhood memories of church prayer, especially the liturgy, which are the best. To return to these memories after all that I have lived through here, in the evening of my life and free of passion, to plunge wholeheartedly into the sea of beauty we experience in the church, to be refreshed by it, that is what I really long for.

I know that the lack of a place of worship is a terrible privation and a real misfortune, and yet there are so many attractive possibilities outside the church. Perhaps it is idiotic of me, but that is what I think and I must say so. So I read a lot here, and sometimes listen to Beethoven, Mozart, Tchaikovsky or Borodin. But these are really only surrogates, and I think that if I were free there would not be a single moment available, for I would devote myself fully to the beauty of the church.

Work is work and always exhausting, yet it is not as bad as it was last year with the quota of ten cubic metres. I remember it with horror. What is more, the weather is still unusually warm and windless. It is a beautiful start to winter.

From the moral viewpoint work is relaxing and calming. But what is difficult to tolerate is the permanently harrowing life in the hut, with its noise, its constant frightful women-fixated swearing, and its whole torrents of filth defiling the air, an air I have been breathing now for five years.

Early this morning I saw the northern lights; they are not as bright here as at Solovky, but nevertheless beautiful.

Nadvoitsy
18 December 1935

I send you very best wishes for Christmas. Another year gone by, and yet another feast day . . .

Here everything is as usual, except that I have received a rejection of my application from the local authorities. But it has been explained to me that I can apply again in a month's time with better chance of success. Refusal has nothing to do with antipathy to me personally – my credentials were entirely in order – but with general considerations concerning people of my sort. In short, it will be as he who leads us wills it. One should not be prey to any illusions.

I have been sent half a skin of fur. Here it is still very warm, two to three degrees. I am reading Gogol.

Nadvoitsy
28 March 1936

Christos voskresse! Christ has risen! Today is Good Friday. How I long for the church service! The uncertainty, the separation and the waiting is causing me such pain . . .

Nadvoitsy
26 May 1936

I have some news: unexpectedly I was taken off general duties and was made industrial statistician in the technical production department. There will be no lack of work: in front of me I can see a sea of all sorts of figures. I will try not to drown in it. On the other hand I can recuperate a little physically. I am in good health, and the weather is good.

Nadvoitsy
23 January 1937

In my external life there have been one or two changes for the worse. I am again in the hut with the plank bunk beds built on the "railway carriage" system, in the camp that you saw from a distance. There are a lot of people here, quite different ones, and it is noisy and tedious. I am still doing the same work, but now I have to work more in the evening. All this oppresses and annoys me: another proof of my spiritual weakness and immaturity.

Nadvoitsy
6 February 1937

Long before it happened I used to think how dreadful it would be if your Mama died before you did. I worried far more about you than about her. The dreadful agony of her death will have compounded your pain.

During her suffering people told you that in face of such agony one could lose one's faith. I think that the hearts of those who said this have had no real experience of the Cross nor its secrets. The suffering of the innocent one, the agony of his death, the Cross which, face to face with eternity, he took upon himself, this is the foundation of our understanding of the world and of our faith. The view that suffering is punishment for personal sins is totally unchristian, and is already refuted in the Book of Job. For according to our faith suffering is transformation, it is transfiguration of the world in its entirety and participation in the divine plan of creation. We tend to judge superficially and only see the external wrapping of life, and are unaware of those deep layers of existence where real events and changes take place.

A single beautiful thought, a single devout feeling or an effort pleasing to God can effect a greater transformation in life, indeed in the cosmos, than any external event, however massive, even though such change remains in- visible to the outer eye which is only aware of externals.

When he was nailed to the cross and killed by the world, surely it was clear to everyone around him that this suffering was not only undeserved and monstrous but also senseless. Yet it was precisely this suffering which saved the world and brought final victory over death.

You write that the physical suffering transformed your mother into a single frenzied cry of pain.

Please excuse me, but from your report I receive quite a different impression. Surely her words of suffering and pain in the last hours of her life, "My God, what pain!" are also the expression of absolute faith, humility, patience and the highest level of spiritual life. We must remember him again, and that his suffering on the cross also expressed itself in the cry, "My God, my God!" Was not this death-cry the living witness of his absolute divine humanity?

You ask if you will ever meet the deceased again; your heart, you say, hesitates to abandon itself totally to the consolation of faith. Is it our affair to doubt it? The experience of love, the whole experience of the Church since Christ rose from the dead is a sure pledge for our hope. This future encounter is less in doubt than our own existence, an encounter where we shall recognise and love one another in a way impossible on earth. But there is more: for that event is not only what we hope for but is also the true goal of our lives. Each twist of our emotions, each thought, each wish and desire will influence the great and invisible mysteries of the world. They all bring nearer the time of transformation, the time of the transfiguration of the world (or conversely push it further away). And suffering, too, is a means whereby we can assist the creative act of the universe.

I know how infinitely difficult it is for you, how much your heart is bleeding. I also know that such suffering is inescapable and inevitable. How much I like to think that it will help the deceased on her new journey in the world beyond. I hope these words of comfort will be of benefit. Bow down to the ground for me at the grave of the one we loved.

Nadvoitsy
22 February 1937

I am tired the whole time and my head aches badly. Recently I received a written answer to my frequent enquiries about the length of my imprisonment. They reckon that on 1.1.36 I had done 2190 days. If everything goes well I will be released as we assumed about the end of 1939. Till then it is still a long time, but at least it is a ray of light. God help me survive that long.

Nadvoitsy
7 April 1937

Christ has risen!

Perhaps these lines will reach you on Easter Eve. My heart is not ready for it. The rush of life, my lassitude, my darkness of soul and my overwhelming grief about past and present events have prevented me from dressing it up as festively as I should. Yet I believe that he is thinking of me and supports me in his love, even when my heart is dark and faint. I remember how he visited and consoled me after many difficult days in my cell.

Nadvoitsy
18 April 1937

Christ has risen!

I have spent these days in sadness and confusion and in grief and longing, with no one near whom I know well. It is now the ninth time that I have not spent Easter Eve buoyed up by the waves of church beauty, but have had to experience it from the shore. So many people I have known have died, and our earthly paths will never cross again. Finally there is much here which is difficult to endure, there is lots of noise and inane hustle and bustle. The people in the hut where I am at present are not bad, but simply so noisy.

I spent Easter Saturday in a state of agitation. When evening came a cold rain fell, and the dark river was still covered here and there by ice which is now breaking up. Behind this the dark outlines of the trees were visible, and I paced around the camp yard in this damp twilight.

"Everything lies in God's hand"

Nadvoitsy
29 May 1937

Leaving Nadvoitsy. Where I am going I do not know. Will let you know at the first opportunity.

Uroksa
7 June 1937

Imagine a crystal clear Karelian summer, where day and night blend into an unbroken triumph of light, which sometimes warms you, almost burns you, then cools you again, but which never goes out. All around us is Lake Vyg, and behind us the forest. I am on a small patch of land, the island of Uroksa. But do not imagine that this Finnish name has anything to do with the Russian "Urka" (thief, bandit). There is absolutely none of that sort of people here, merely "law breakers" like myself.

I am on general duties, that is, handling wood and removing bark. I can cope very well with the physical aspect, but it is the quotas which I cannot maintain. I am working night shift and get back from work in the morning, and then go to sleep outside for it is far healthier than in the hut. It is so good to sleep under an open sky and to take in deep breaths of the fresh morning air; it is a real idyll here in this respect and I am lucky and very pleased. I fear that there may be problems with the delivery of letters and parcels, for the railway station is eighteen kilometres away, sixteen on foot and two by boat.

Uroksa
14 June 1937

There is no longer any doubt that the term of my

imprisonment has not been calculated from the beginning. It is true I have not yet received official confirmation, but as I said, it cannot be doubted. So we must set the day of my release for 10 November 1940 (for my forty days of imprisonment in Kiev have never been included in it). I am now reconciled to this, for I never had much faith in the arithmetic behind the calculations . . .

Uroksa,
26 June 1937

I am writing a few hours before our journey continues. I am leaving Uroksa tomorrow morning. Where am I going to? Evidently it is far away, beyond the White Sea Canal area. Our group is calm and a pleasant one to travel with. I am in good shape physically and mentally. Everything is entrusted to his will.

Lake Uros
29 July 1937

For three days now I have been leading a strange bivouac existence. I left my Uroksa and have arrived at a unit on Lake Uros. Yesterday we spent the whole day travelling and today there has been a lot of excitement as we have been preparing for the rest of the journey. I am equipping myself for an endlessly long journey to the end of the world . . .

However because of my lack of physical fitness I have been left behind with several others, and tomorrow I must return to Uroksa. There is no way I can avoid another journey, but at least it will not be as long.

"Everything lies in God's hand"

Uroksa,
2 August 1937

I am back in Uroksa. The few days of my absence fled by. Our "excursion" did not go too badly. On a beautiful sunny day we set out in the direction of Lake Uros, at first by boat and then on foot. Then evening came, and then night, which we spent bivouacing in railway station mood, impatient for the next stage and preparing for the continuation of our voyage while listening to a multitude of rumours. The idea of travel contains something powerful and gripping. Even when the conditions are as odd as they are with us . . .

Uroksa
24 September 1937

My hut is nothing like the one in which you visited me. Can you imagine my life at present? Can you imagine my upper bunk where I have the enormous advantage of being on my own with nobody next to me? And the noisy activity in the hut, where games smack of swearing and human sorrow, where here and there the beauty of a soul shines through? Can you imagine the mornings when I wake to the metallic clank of the piece of railway track and step out of the hut and look over the lake and into the distance? Whether the sky is dim or leaden, or whether it is lit for the last time with an autumn azure, what the lake is like, whether ruffled white or smooth and transparent as it sometimes is: this is what makes the day. The ten hours' work can be tolerated under a friendly sky with the sun shining, but in icy rain it is torture, especially of course when one is outside and the cold and the wet penetrate the boots and the feet and the hands. In the evening after work there is food and then roll call, and in the hut there is the buzz of voices, but I sit for an hour or so on my upper bunk, leafing through a book and trying to be alone with my thoughts and memories.

Only later, when the hut is asleep, do I climb down from my "hide" and pace about in thought. At night I leave the hut and admire the flickering northern lights.

I am in good health and spirits.

Uroksa
12 October 1937

I continue in good health and spirits. Some changes have taken place, but . . . if God allows it . . . I'll write about it all later . . . at present I am not working.

28 October 1937

Am in good health and spirits. Not yet been given work. Am calm at heart. Do not worry if my letters are late.

10 November 1937

Do not be upset or worried that I write so rarely. I am in good health and spirits. Perhaps I shall write more frequently soon, and at greater length.

In December 1937 the correspondence broke off.

July 1940: "Having committed a further crime, condemned to ten years' strict isolation with no right to receive or to write letters."

1943: Same notification received.

August 1955: The following official communication arrived from Petrozavodsk: "Anatoly Yevgenyevitch Shurakovski died in the hospital of the Petrozavodsk prison on 10 October 1939 of tuberculosis complicated by a lung infection."

6

"Be filled through and through with eternity"

From the sermons of Archimandrite Tavrion

Archimandrite Tavrion, who died on 13 August 1978, was father confessor at the Monastery of the Transfiguration near Riga. "Many people went to him, many were consoled by him, he gave assistance to many, including also material assistance, and now that he has died there are many orphans," writes Father Dmitry Dudko, editor of his sermons and of reminiscences of him. The following texts "appeared" in a religious samizdat journal. Unfortunately they contain no bio- graphical detail.

The Divine Liturgy begins with the words, "The Lamb of God which taketh away the sins of the world is slain for the life and salvation of the world." The slaying of the Lamb of God is our re-birth. We bear a great responsibility for other people; and we must offer them something great as well, and there is no more effective way of saying thanks to God than through the Divine Liturgy. It is a thanksgiving, and we are showing God our gratitude through it.

Therefore it is not to be seen as an act of repentance but of gratitude that the Lord has taken our sins upon himself and the Lamb has been slain for us. We can only contemplate this Lamb, feel his influence and thank him, for he bears the sins of the whole world. This is why we are all gathered together here in the church in liturgical prayer, for it can effect so much. It is because of this prayer that the whole universe can live. And if this prayer can carry the Whole, how easy it is for each of us to save our souls! In doing this we are not standing there in supplication, poor and oppressed: no, the Lamb has been slain for you. And it is nothing less than the Son of God! In the Liturgy we are participating in the ceremony of a divine banquet, the wedding banquet of God's beloved Son. All this takes place so that we shall become worthy. Let us imagine someone going to a wedding, imagine the pleasure and satisfaction. And remember too the magnificence of a dish which is presented with love. Here the Lord is serving us himself and is offering himself to us. That is why towards the end of the Liturgy, before the Communion, the following words are directed at those who step forward to take the Cup: "The holy things unto them that are holy!" What an exhilarating pronouncement! The holy are called upon to receive the holy. That is how it is. For the priest takes confession and forgives you your sins on the strength of the grace which has been bestowed upon him. When you believe in this forgiveness then you are already holy. Hence the call, "The holy things unto them that are holy!"

You have gathered here from many different places, each with your own troubles. As you know, all of us strive for peace of mind. We seek it and find it in our faith, in our prayer, and in receiving the sacraments. And those, too, who live far outside the influence of the Church are also seeking peace where they can find it. Our way of life encourages the search for peace. See how modern society lives in large noisy cities and yet people like to relax somewhere in the calm of unspoiled nature. What does it mean? It means that the human soul is seeking its own unspoiled beauty, a beauty which is in character with it. Religion, the Church of God and the Gospels represent a beauty which accords precisely. Our souls are revealed through the Gospels, which are the inner sanctum of the soul. If you are aware of your soul and recognise in it a quality which links it with the Heavenly Father then you will understand the Gospels. To have the Gospels to hand is a rare piece of good fortune, for they reveal the truth to you. Outwardly they look modest, yet they contain the answer to the whole world. There has never existed such a wonder on earth. So many states and nations have risen and then fallen without trace, but the Gospels continue to exist. They preach to all nations and in all tongues. And when a person seeks the truth he sets out to study the word of God, whether as a believer or unbeliever. Why? Because if you do not know the Gospels you are totally ignorant and illiterate. In the world there is a lot which is beautiful and of material and spiritual value: where does it all come from? From the Gospels. So can someone who loves technology or science or art or literature ignore them? No.

God's word is always beautiful, and very special by nature. The Gospels are particularly accessible to the minds of children, and hence it used to be said that Christianity was the religion of old women and children. Children grasp the laws of being intuitively: they understand the word of God with absolute immediacy and accuracy. You parents, you must not deprive your children of this. Your duty is to sow goodness and love in them. Bearing children is a matter for nature, but raising them is a matter for parents. Educate them! They have heart, a will of their own and a sense of freedom, and your task is not an easy one. Do not offend them, for you love them and are seeking joy and consolation through them, but at the same time remember your responsibility. Your treatment of them in their earliest childhood will determine the rest of their lives. See what a mighty responsibility you bear! Conditions and upbringing can transform a beautiful child into an ugly and terrible one.

Our Saviour said, "I am the door of the sheepfold" (John 10:7). That means that it is only through Christ that one can enter life, and whoever does not go through Christ, through his door, is a thief and a robber. "He that entereth not by the door into the fold of the sheep but climbeth up some other way, the same is a thief and a robber" (John 10:1). Think about this and try to understand it. How well the Lord admonishes us, and how firmly! See, the priest is a thief and a robber, the monk is a priest and a robber, and you parents are so too if we do not atune our lives to the Gospels and are not aware of our responsibility towards them. So, brothers and sisters in Christ, think hard about your love for the Gospels. If you have this love, then the inner sanctum of your being will be revealed. The Lord assist you!

What are you hoping for? What are you expecting? Indeed what can you expect as long as you are surrounded by people who live without faith in God? Look at their pitiful existence: at first sight it seems that their lives are easy, for they are young, well educated, and they live well. But see how empty their way of life is! It is dreadful to see them, but nevertheless we know that they are living in fear, and that we are responsible for them. Can you see what is being demanded of us? We must not only maintain our own faith but also show it to others: "The time for teaching the faith is over: now we must show it." Everyone who thinks themselves Christian should consider their position and ask themselves what they are doing, for the consolation of faith, whatever their walk in life. We have been transposed back in the time of the Apostles, and the Apostles never had any other prospect than the sufferings of Christ. Their lives, too, ended in serious affliction, for some were beheaded, and others were crucified or thrown to the wild beasts to be eaten. The first Christians also lived this way, fearing the approaching day, wondering whether they would be thrown to the animals or their children taken from them and torn to pieces. For three hundred years Christians were obliged to live like this. What gave them support and what confirmed their faith? It was their knowledge of the truth and the certainty of their faith. And it is the same today: when someone is filled with the necessity of faith he will find it and retain it.

Yet our world is such that a believer is hardly accepted as normal. If he cannot be dissuaded from his faith he is put in a mental asylum. So how should we conduct ourselves? Consider what value we must accord the grace which God has given us. With the help of the Liturgy, which is heaven on earth, and with the help of the Cup, we can find peace of mind and can strengthen our faith and be filled through and through with eternity. It is important that we and others are aware of this possibility. Brothers and sisters! Today everyone can read and write, so read the word of God and through it God's spirit will come to you and you will be saved, as it is said in church: "Each soul is given life by the Holy Ghost." Soon we shall be celebrating the Mid-Easter Season[1] in which the Gospels relate that the Lord speaks wonderfully of the living water: "He that believeth in me, as the Scripture hath said, out of his belly shall flow rivers of living water" (John 7:38). He is speaking of the faithful filled with the Holy Ghost. When we have this water in us we are saved and can save those around us. The Lord grant us strength to achieve this!

NOTES

Preface

1 Zoya Krakhmalnikova was released from exile on 29 June 1987 and now lives with her husband in Moscow.

2 Startsy (*sing.* starets): holy men, often monks, of the Russian church in the eighteenth and nineteenth centuries. They are generally associated with the contemplative life and much respected for their gifts of spiritual guidance.

3 F. Schuon: "Der Sinn für das Heilige" [The Sense of the Sacred], *Bannkreis des Heiligen, Herderbücherei-Initiative*, 67 (1986).

4 M. Picard: *The Flight from God* (London: Harvill Press, 1951).

5 See F. Rötzer: *French Philosophers* (Boer, 1986).

The Historical Background

1 D. Popielovsky: *The Russian Church under the Soviet Regime, 1917-1982* (New York, 1984), vol. 1, p. 177.

2 *Russkie pravoslavnye ierarchi. Ispovedniki i mučeniki* (Paris: YMCA Press, 1986).

3 Ibid. p. 38.

4 This tradition is discussed in R. M. French ed.: *The Way of a Pilgrim* (London: Triangle, 1986).

Chapter 1

1 Professor S. R. Sheviryov (1806-64): professor, literary critic and poet at Moscow University.

Chapter 2

1 The Church of the One Faith: a section of the Old Believers which retained its rituals from the time of Patriarch Nikhon's reform (1654). In 1806 it was recognised by the Orthodox Church.

2 Seraphim of Zarov (1760-1833): one of the greatest ascetics and spiritual leaders of the modern Russian church.

3 Sergiev Possad: now Zagorsk.

4 Shurenka: nickname for Alexandra.

5 John of Kronstadt (Ioann Ilyich Sergiev), 1829-1908: a Russian Orthodox mystic and preacher. He was known for the power of his prayer and the intensity of his experience of the liturgy. His social activity earned him the respect of all sections of society. Csar Alexander III received the last rites from him.

6 This is probably the prayer of repentence of St Andrew of Crete which is read in the evening service on the Thursday of the fifth week of fasting.

7 This is probably a reference to the prayer of the priest in the Russian Orthodox requiem mass: "Grant, O Lord, rest unto the souls of thy departed servants, in a place of refreshment, light and peace, from whence pain, sorrow and sighing flee away".

8 Yekaterina: Katherine of Sinai.

9 A quotation from an evening prayer which is also sung at Easter: "God will rise up, and may his enemies scatter and those that hate him disperse before his face. May they drift away like smoke".

Chapter 3

1 Menaion: book of divine service for the immovable feasts in the Church calendar, containing among other things the lives of the saints. Triodion: liturgical book of the great period of fasting, including Easter week.

2 Amvrosy (A. M. Grenkov): a renowned monk and starets at the Optino monastery. People of every age and standing sought spiritual guidance from him. He was the model for Dostoevsky's starets Zossima in *The Brothers Karamazov*.

Chapter 4

1 Massya: a childhood name with which Bishop German sometimes referred to himself in his letters.

2 Mama: Vera Timofeyeva, to whom letters from the Bishop are addressed.

3 Sergievo or Sergiev Possad: now Zagorsk.

4 Tanya: a nun who accompanied Bishop German in his first exile and helped provide for other exiled and imprisoned bishops.

5 Komsomol: Young Communist League.

6 Slava: Brother of Natalia V.

7 Vanya: Father Israil, Abbot of the Gethsemane Monastery.

8 Father Potapy: A monk at the Holy Trinity Monastery.

9 Danilov: Abbot Fyodor (Posdneyevsky) of the Moscow Danilov Monastery.

10 Krotky: Bishop Nikodim (Krotky).

11 A reference to the end of his exile.

12 Fedya: Bishop Fyodor (Posdneyevski).

13 Vitya: the author's brother Bishop Varlam (Victor Stepanovitch Ryashentzev).

14 Father Michey: a monk at the Holy Trinity Monastery.

15 Grandfather: a conspiratorial name for the Patriarch
   Tikhon.

16 6 December: Feast day of St Mitrofan, first Bishop of
   Voronezh (1623- 1702).

17 Lartshik: Bishop Hilarion (Belyski). This is a reference to
   the Solovki camp.

18 Zossima: the Solovki camp.

Chapter 5

1 The Sviri camps were on the river Svir, between the
  Lagoda and Onega lakes, north-east of Leningrad. In the
  1930s three hydroelectric power stations were built there
  with the help of prisoners.

2 Paragraph 58 became known as the "political" paragraph.
  Section 6: "Espionage". Section 11: "Aggravating
  circumstances connected with any sort of crime".

3 The Tolstoy-Datche camp was for sick prisoners,
  twenty-five kilometres from the Dyedi railway station.

4 Saint Ignatius (d AD 110): Bishop of Antioch. His seven
  letters, written on the way to his martyrdom in Rome,
  give valuable insight into the early Christian Church.

5 Michail Vassilyevich Nesterov (1862-1942): a religious
  symbolist and historical painter.

6 The Spring of St Nicholas. On 9 May the Eastern Church
  celebrates the transfer of the Saint's relics from Myra to
  Bari. This is in addition to 6 December, the other feast
  day of the Saint.

Chapter 6

1 Mid-Easter Season: Wednesday of the fourth week after
  Easter.

Hope and Suffering
Desmond Tutu

"Here . . . is the authentic voice of Christian prophecy in our day. Unafraid to proclaim . . . the truth about apartheid . . . to challenge . . . the assault on human rights . . . to risk the consequences for himself . . . But always in hope: always in love: always in the certainty that God is present . . ."

Trevor Huddleston

Naught for Your Comfort
Trevor Huddleston

The book that foretold the Soweto uprising and stirred the conscience of the world . . .

Instrument of Thy Peace
Alan Paton

"Worthy of a permanent place on the short shelf of enduring classics of the life of the Spirit."

Henry P. Van Dusan,
Union Theological Seminary

Let My People Go
Albert Luthuli

"Luthuli's love for his country transcends his loyalty to any one racial group within it. This book will surely convince the world that the Nobel Prize was most justly awarded to its author."

Trevor Huddleston

Fount Paperbacks

Fount is one of the leading paperback publishers of religious books and below are some of its recent titles.

- ☐ FRIENDSHIP WITH GOD David Hope £2.95
- ☐ THE DARK FACE OF REALITY Martin Israel £2.95
- ☐ LIVING WITH CONTRADICTION Esther de Waal £2.95
- ☐ FROM EAST TO WEST Brigid Marlin £3.95
- ☐ GUIDE TO THE HERE AND HEREAFTER
  Lionel Blue/Jonathan Magonet £4.50
- ☐ CHRISTIAN ENGLAND (1 Vol) David Edwards £10.95
- ☐ MASTERING SADHANA Carlos Valles £3.95
- ☐ THE GREAT GOD ROBBERY George Carey £2.95
- ☐ CALLED TO ACTION Fran Beckett £2.95
- ☐ TENSIONS Harry Williams £2.50
- ☐ CONVERSION Malcolm Muggeridge £2.95
- ☐ INVISIBLE NETWORK Frank Wright £2.95
- ☐ THE DANCE OF LOVE Stephen Verney £3.95
- ☐ THANK YOU, PADRE Joan Clifford £2.50
- ☐ LIGHT AND LIFE Grazyna Sikorska £2.95
- ☐ CELEBRATION Margaret Spufford £2.95
- ☐ GOODNIGHT LORD Georgette Butcher £2.95
- ☐ GROWING OLDER Una Kroll £2.95

All Fount Paperbacks are available at your bookshop or newsagent, or they can be ordered by post from Fount Paperbacks, Cash Sales Department, G.P.O. Box 29, Douglas, Isle of Man. Please send purchase price plus 22p per book, maximum postage £3. Customers outside the UK send purchase price, plus 22p per book. Cheque, postal order or money order. No currency.

NAME (Block letters) _____

ADDRESS_____

_____

_____